FOUNDATIONS OF MODERN PSYCHOLOGY SERIES
Richard S. Lazarus, *Editor*

JULIAN E. HOCHBERG

Professor, Department of Psychology at Cornell University; author and researcher in the related fields of perception, attention, and nonverbal communication.

Perception

PRENTICE-HALL, INC., *Englewood Cliffs, New Jersey*

PERCEPTION, *Julian E. Hochberg*

PRENTICE-HALL FOUNDATIONS
OF MODERN PSYCHOLOGY SERIES

Richard S. Lazarus, *Editor*

PRENTICE-HALL INTERNATIONAL, INC., *London*
PRENTICE-HALL OF AUSTRALIA, PTY., LTD., *Sydney*
PRENTICE-HALL OF CANADA, LTD., *Toronto*
PRENTICE-HALL OF INDIA PRIVATE LIMITED, *New Delhi*
PRENTICE-HALL OF JAPAN, INC., *Tokyo*
PRENTICE-HALL DE MEXICO, S.A., *Mexico City*

Designed by Harry Rinehart
Drawings by Lorelle Raboni

C-65690(p), C-65691(c)

Foundations
of Modern Psychology
Series

The tremendous growth and vitality of psychology and its increasing fusion with the social and biological sciences demand a new approach to teaching at the introductory level. The basic course, geared as it usually is to a single text that tries to skim everything—that sacrifices depth for superficial breadth—is no longer adequate. Psychology has become too diverse for any one man, or a few men, to write about with complete authority. The alternative, a book that ignores many essential areas in order to present more comprehensively and effectively a particular aspect or view of psychology, is also insufficient. For in this solution, many key areas are simply not communicated to the student at all.

The Foundations of Modern Psychology is a new and different approach to the introductory course. The instructor is offered a series of short volumes, each a self-contained book on the special issues, methods, and content of a basic topic by a noted authority who is actively contributing to that particular field. And taken together, the volumes cover the full scope of psychological thought, research, and application.

The result is a series that offers the advantage of tremendous flexibility and scope. The teacher can choose the subjects he wants to emphasize and present them in the order he desires. And without necessarily sacrificing breadth, he can provide the student with a much fuller treatment of individual areas at the introductory level than is normally possible. If he does not have time to include all the volumes in his course, he can recommend the omitted ones as outside reading, thus covering the full range of psychological topics.

Psychologists are becoming increasingly aware of the importance of reaching the introductory student with high-quality, well-written, and stimulating material, material that highlights the continuing and exciting search for new knowledge. The Foundations of Modern Psychology Series is our attempt to place in the hands of instructors the best textbook tools for this purpose.

Preface

Perception is one of the oldest subjects of speculation and research in the study of man, with a correspondingly long history of theory and fact. I have tried to keep this brief introduction open to new approaches and possibilities, but at the same time conservative—as a science must be if it is to profit from the inquiry of previous centuries.

This dual aim requires a rather condensed treatment of this increasingly technical discipline; however, details are presented only in the context of the broader questions that make them important, and the more demanding material has been collected in plates that may be skipped without serious loss to the over-all discussion. Figures in this latter category are: 4-16, 4-25, 4-26, 4-27, 4-28, 5-1B and C, and 5-12. With these exceptions, the figures and their captions should be treated as integral parts of the text, since pictorial display has been used mainly as a substitute for (not as a supplement to) written exposition.

The reader is also urged to follow the order of the chapters, since there is a close development from one to the next as we pursue the general question of "Why things look as they do."

Julian E. Hochberg

Contents

Contents

ix

Contents

The Study of Perception

We study perception in an attempt to explain our observations of the world around us. Some of the reasons for undertaking this study are specific and practical. Some are general and theoretical, and arise out of the very old problem of how man comes to know his world.

In fact, the study of perception started long before a science of psychology existed. A great deal of the early research in this area was the work of physiologists and physicists, and many important contributions to perceptual psychology were made by men who are not usually thought of as psychologists. This is still true today because

1

the problems of perception cut across other sciences: We cannot begin to understand man's perception of the world unless we also understand something about the world as a set of physical events and about man as a physiological structure.

It is not enough to say that the study of *perception* is concerned with the observation of the world: so are physics, chemistry, and all the other sciences. Moreover, as we shall see, these physical sciences are capable of completely explaining the world and everything in it—at least in principle. Why, then, do we need a separate study of *perception*? We may first become concerned about the perceptual process in the following kinds of problems:

1. *When our observation turns out to be in error* and damaging accidents occur (misjudging an aircraft landing or automobile traffic conditions) or awkward social situations develop (mistaking somebody's *anger* for *joy*). Such occasions of mistaken perceptions and *illusions* (in which there are discrepancies between the observed world and the physical world) call for the study of the processes responsible for our observations. The general question of the trustworthiness of our "senses" has intrigued philosophers for centuries. More prosaically, many persons in technical professions (such as traffic safety engineers) are concerned with eliminating misperceptions, and at least as many are concerned with causing them—beauticians, fashion designers, and, above all, artists.

2. *When we want to replace the real world, by some specially prepared substitutes* (or *surrogates*) such as pictures, TV, or hi-fi, to which observers will respond as they would have responded to the real objects or events.

3. *When we want to be able to replace a human observer by a machine.* In this case, we must first find out exactly what the machine has to do if it were to replace, say, a human plane-spotter, map-reader, or apple-sorter. Frequently, only the end result is important: The automatic door-opener at the supermarket does not have to *see* you in the same way a doorman does in order to do its job. If, however, our purpose is to show that we really understand how observers, as human mechanisms, operate, we must first examine the perceptual process in great detail in order to know what we are trying to simulate.

4. *When we wish to discover the bodily processes upon which our observations depend.* For example, when we seek to understand and remedy sensory defects (such as poor vision or hearing), we must study how our sensory organs contribute to our perception of the world.

Perception, Physics, and Psychology

Most people realize that the sense organs must function properly in order for perception to occur, but they usually assume that the organs furnish the brain with copies of the external world. This is not so. There are knotty philosophical issues involved in this question, but here we raise the point more modestly to call attention to certain characteristic differences between the physical world and the perceived world.

There are vast differences between the "real," or physical, world, as it is defined and measured by the instruments of physical science, and the perceived world of normal, unaided observation.* Four kinds of difference will be important to us in this book:

1. Many physical events cannot be observed at all by the unaided sense organs: the too-large, the too-small, and the energies for which we lack sensory organs, such as damaging radiation from cosmic rays or from the fall-out of nuclear explosions. Physical science needs instruments to detect what our senses cannot. (We shall discuss these limitations in Chapter 2, pp. 8–10, 14). The reverse is also true. There are numerous properties for which no physical instruments can be presently devised, such as tastiness, sexual attractiveness, and artistic quality.

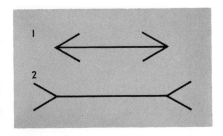

Figure 1-1. Perceived length vs. measured length. The Mueller-Lyer pattern shown here is an "illusion": Are lines 1 and 2 of equal length? As measured by some physical instrument (a ruler, for example), they are both about one inch in length. As observed without such aids, 1 appears shorter than 2.

2. What we observe is never in *exact* correspondence with the physical situation. Some aspects are omitted, some added, some distorted. An *illusion* exists when observations made with the aid of physical instruments yield different results from those made without such instruments. (See Figure 1-1; we shall discuss illusions in Chapter 4, pp. 54–57.) In fact, most of the qualities of the world we do perceive (*size, color, weight,* and so on) are only very loosely related to the physical measurements to which we have given the same names.

Even if an event is capable of affecting our sensory organs, there is no guarantee that we will observe it: We first must look at an object before we can see it. In addition, we may not even be able to see what we *do* attend to: Certain "organizational" requirements must be met. These are not easy to explain at this point, but we shall discuss them in Chapters 4 and 5. For now, though, we can illustrate this principle. Look at Figure 1-2A. It contains a picture of an old woman. Each of its parts is as much above the *threshold* of the sense organs as are those of the young woman (in fact, they are the same parts doing double duty). Can you see it? Can

* I do not intend to imply that the physical world is more or less "real" than the perceived world, since the term "reality" has no specific scientific meaning; however, the physical world does have certain exceedingly useful consistencies that, as we shall see, the perceived world does not always display—and vice versa.

you read the hieroglyphics in Figure 1-2B? If you turn to footnotes A and B on page 15, you will then be able to observe these previously invisible objects.

For advertising or courting purposes, it is desirable to be highly visible. For concealing oneself from unfriendly eyes, it is good to be invisible. Both man and nature have developed effective techniques for achieving these ends (Figure 1-2C, D).

In short, the perceived world is not identical to the world we learn about through physical measures, and one of the primary tasks of the study of perception is to discover the relationship between them. This study cannot be a *purely* psychological discipline because physics and mathematics are needed to determine what physical energies act upon our sense organs, and physiological and anatomical factors set the limits of what *can* affect the sensory organs. On the other hand, no amount of study of the physical energies alone, or the physiological structure alone, will teach us anything about perception.

The study of perception is *primarily* psychological. In fact, the problems of perception were once central to all other fields of study in psychology. Until the early part of this century, the main aim of psychology was to explain all of the possible thoughts or ideas we have by their origin in past and present

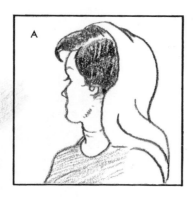

Figure 1-2. Objects may be physically present, yet they may not be observable. (A) Can you see the old woman? (After Boring.) Every part is clearly visible. (B) Can you read the symbols in the row? (C) Natural self-efface-ment: "protective coloration." (D) Artificial invisibility: man-made camou-flage.

sensory experience (pp. 32–45). This goal has been pretty well abandoned, and perception has vacated the central position it once maintained. As a discipline in its own right, however, perception is still usually regarded as "basic," even though the attempt to rest all of psychology upon it is no longer seriously entertained.

We shall discuss the topic of perception only as a set of scientific problems, that is, as problems that are accessible to factual statement of the questions and to factual evaluation of the answers. This approach leaves out a lot of what has been said on the subject. At the same time, we shall try to consider research problems and findings in terms of their relevance to either practical application, or the furtherance of coherent human knowledge, or both.

In Chapters 2 and 3 we shall survey the study of how we perceive very simple physical phenomena, such as a spot of light of a particular wavelength. Many psychologists still view the results of such research as the basic groundwork on which our other perceptual knowledge must rest. Otherwise, this research is mainly of interest to sensory physiologists, and to human engineers who design signal lights, instrument panels, and so on.

In Chapter 4 we shall consider attempts to use these findings to explain how we perceive the world, and the difficulties that confront these attempts. The objects studied here and in Chapter 5 are still "physical"—sizes, distances, lightnesses—but they are closer to the world of normal observation, and they are of more general interest, especially to artists and educators.

Chapter 6 samples the new field of social perception. The objects studied here include people, their social relationships, and their personal qualities, all of which are of potential interest to social psychologists, advertisers, and theatrical directors. Although research in this area is very sparse, its promise is great.

By following this organization, which is roughly the historical order in which investigation has proceeded, experimental research appears in the context of its purposes, and the objects of perception become increasingly more natural and meaningful from one section to the next.

Because the different senses have not been equally explored, and because they are not equally important for the questions asked in each of our sections, we shall not treat one sensory system at a time. Instead, we shall first survey the sense of sight, and then introduce the others as problems necessitate. This source of distraction may be relieved somewhat because vision will predominate throughout, reflecting both the importance of visual perception and the ease of presenting visual phenomena on the printed page.

Wherever possible, I have presented miniature experiments to illustrate important phenomena and to circumvent more lengthy descriptions. You are urged to perform these experiments, and thus to transform an abstract discussion into concrete participation.

The Sensations
and Their Measurement

We observe the world through our several senses, or *modalities of sensation*. Imagine that a songstress is performing: If you close your eyes, the song continues, but you can no longer tell whether the songstress is blonde or brunette; if the sight was more pleasing than the sound, you can reopen your eyes and plug your ears with your fingers. It is easy in most cases to separate the sensory channels of seeing and hearing. But some of the other senses are not so easy to separate. For example, taste and smell are closely intertwined (so that pinching the nostrils or catching a cold results in truly surprising losses in

6

2

flavor), and the position senses, as we shall see, are almost inseparably involved in the operation of seeing and hearing.

Here is a listing of the major senses. Those that will engage us in this book are marked with asterisks. Note that there are more than the traditional "five senses."

1. *The distance senses:* seeing * and hearing.*
2. *The skin senses:* touch,* warmth, cold, pain, and the closely related chemical senses of taste and smell.
3. *The deep senses:* position * and motion * of muscles and joints (kinesthesis), the senses of equilibration * (vestibular), and the senses of the internal organs.

For each of our senses, we have specialized sense organs that are most readily aroused to physiological activity by one class of physical energy or *stimulation,* and whose resulting action or *response* allows us to detect or *discriminate* the presence or absence of that physical energy, and produces the corresponding characteristic experience. Thus, although we can tell that there is intense sunshine on the skin of our shoulders by its warmth (and by its subsequent blisters), the eye is immensely more sensitive to the presence or absence of light-energy than that, and only the eye's response produces the experience of light or darkness.

But we can tell much more about the world than that it is light or dark, noisy or silent. With each sense organ, we can make many different observations: We observe that lights differ in degree or amount, not only in their presence or absence, and that they differ in other ways as well. Within each separate sense, these differences in quality and quantity seem to recur in various combinations in the objects we observe around us—qualities such as "blue," "red," "cold," "hard," and so on. To discover that light-energy is the physical stimulus for the observation of "light" vs. "dark," and that the eye is the receptive sense organ is relatively simple, but to discover the physical stimuli and the anatomical equipment that are responsible for the different observations we can make *within* each modality of sensation presents far more challenging and fundamental problems.

Two quite different sets of procedures were used to discover the list of different sensory qualities—called *sensations*—that we can observe, and to discover the differences in physical stimuli that are responsible for these differences in sensation. The general procedures were called sensory psychophysics and analytic introspection. We shall examine each of these procedures in some detail, since the first one is still in use, and an understanding of the second is essential in grasping most modern perceptual problems.

PURPOSES AND PRINCIPLES OF SENSORY PSYCHOPHYSICS

The most precise way of cataloguing the "sensations" (that is, the differences we can observe even within each sensory modality) and of discovering their physical bases, is called sensory psychophysics. A measured change is

The Sensations and Their Measurement

made in some single aspect of the physical energy that stimulates a sense organ, in order to find out if this change makes any difference in what the observer perceives. Although each sense organ can do much more than tell us whether or not physical stimulation is present (for example, whether it is day or night), the number of differences we can observe in any sensory modality is limited: Our observations do not change with each and every change in physical stimulation. Just as there are physical energies (like radio waves) that we cannot observe directly because we have no sense organs that are sensitive to them, we cannot observe too-small changes even in those energies for which we do have sense organs. One of the first tasks of sensory psychophysics is to discover what differences we can observe.

The smallest change in any physical stimulation that we can observe with our unaided senses is called the *difference threshold, discrimination threshold,* or *just noticeable difference*—usually abbreviated *JND*. There are several uses for these measures, and a great many *psychophysical methods* have been designed to obtain them.

The Psychophysical Methods and Measures

The psychophysical methods are primarily procedures for measuring thresholds. The concept of thresholds is quite simple, and the psychophysical methods are equally simple —*in principle*. We might measure a difference threshold quite simply by starting with two stimuli that are physically equal, and then change one a little and see whether they still appear equal, change it a little more, and so on, trial by trial, until they are barely different enough physically to appear unequal to each other. The physical difference on the last trial would be the difference threshold.* For example, with two incandescent lamps of the same wattage, we would keep one unchanged, calling it the *standard* stimulus, and increase the voltage of the other lamp, the *variable* stimulus, until its output of light-energy exceeded the difference threshold and it no longer looked identical to the standard but was, instead, just noticeably brighter.

There is a major complication, however. When an observer tries to decide which one of two almost identical objects is brighter (or larger, or heavier, or colder), his judgments fluctuate: Now one looks brighter, now the other. The task is like straining to hear a very faint whispered signal in a hearing test. What first seemed to be a very quiet room now seems to be filled with creaks and echoes, and even the rushing sound of the blood in your own ears makes it difficult to decide whether you actually heard the signal, or whether what you heard was simply a bit of the varying background noise. You might well mistake the background noise for the signal—an error called a *false alarm*— or you might make the opposite mistake, and *miss* the signal. This sort of fluctuating interference afflicts all threshold decisions, so that an observer's relative willingness to commit either false alarms or misses (his so-called *response bias*) will affect the size of the difference threshold. The very nature of the threshold problem demands experimental situations in which the ob-

* If we start with no physical stimulus energy at all, and by small increases discover the smallest quantity that the observer can detect, that quantity (the difference from zero, so to speak) is called the *absolute threshold.*

server cannot be sure of whether he really detects the object he is searching for.*

For these reasons, *the* threshold is not a simple fixed value; it varies over a range of measures, in part because of the varying motivation, attitudes and expectations of the observers. Therefore, more complicated and sophisticated procedures are needed to remove these errors or to allow us to estimate their magnitude, and to decide somewhat arbitrarily on the value of each psychophysical measure. Traditionally, the difference threshold or JND is taken to be the physical stimulus difference between standard and variable that will be detected 50 per cent of the time, that is, the difference that is *just as likely as not* to be discriminated. These thresholds were used to compile the list of stimulus changes that our senses can detect. In addition, however, the thresholds were also used for another and quite different purpose, which we shall consider very briefly.

Psychophysical Laws and Scales

Suppose that we have found the difference threshold at a weight of 100 grams to be 2 grams; that is, with the standard = 100 gm., the JND = 2 gm. We might at first assume that this implies that we can observe as being different any two weights that differ by more than 2 grams. This is not true, however, since the JND changes as we change the standard. Thus, for a standard of 150 grams, the variable would have to be 153 grams to appear just noticeably heavier, and for a standard = 250 gm., the JND = 5 gm. As these results suggest, although the JND is not a constant, the *ratio* of JND/standard is. This law was discovered by E. H. Weber in 1830, and the Weber fraction, JND/standard, is a constant over moderate values of the standard, for a wide variety of stimulation.

When, in this example, the variable of 102 grams is compared with the standard of 100 grams, the variable appears different from the standard in a particular way: It is heavier, and a stimulus of 104 grams will seem heavier than 102 grams; as the weight of the object increases, the sensation of heaviness increases. Similarly in other senses: As the light-energy increases, the light appears brighter; as the sound-pressure waves carry more energy to the ear, the sound gets louder. Here, then, is one way in which sensations change as the stimulating physical energy changes. The magnitude of the sensation increases when the stimulus energy increases. How are the two kinds of increase related? Does doubling the weight in grams result in double the sensa-

---

* In recent years motivation and expectation have been deliberately manipulated to study the problem of how people make difficult decisions—a far cry from the original simple goals for which thresholds were measured. Thus, with rewards of 10¢ for each correct report of a signal, and 5¢ for each report of its absence, and a penalty of 5¢ for each error, the number of false alarms will rise, even though the stimulus is not changed in any way. On the other hand, we can keep both the stimulus and the system of rewards and punishments (called the *payoff function*) constant, and merely change the proportion of *catch trials*—trials on which there really is no difference to be detected. This will change the observer's expectations about how frequently he should be noticing a difference, and again the threshold will change. For a lucid introduction to this new approach to an old technique, see E. Galanter, Contemporary psychophysics. In R. Brown, E. Galanter, E. H. Hess, and G. Mandler, *New directions in psychology*. New York: Holt, Rinehart & Winston, 1962.

tion of heaviness? In order to answer that question, we would need a measuring scale of units of heaviness with which we could tell whether doubling the number of grams of weight, as a physical measure, is observed as doubling the number of those units of heaviness, as a sensation. But how can we construct scales with which to measure sensations? Gustav Theodor Fechner, a physicist and the originator of most of the psychophysical methods, proposed in 1860 that each JND measures an equal increment in sensation and, therefore, that a physical increase of, say, 10 JND's is observed as twice the increase as one of 5 JND's. Taking Weber's law into account (by a mathematical transformation which need not concern us here), this would imply

$$S = C \log M$$

where S = the magnitude of the sensation, M = the physical measure of the stimulus, and C is a constant for a particular sense modality.* Many psychologists however, do not believe that it means anything to talk of "scales of sensation" in this way, and that the only reliable observation that one can make in sensory psychophysics is whether one stimulus appears the same as, or different from, another.

Regardless of whether we agree that within each sensory modality there are scales of intensity or magnitude of sensation that can be measured by the psychophysical methods, there is no question that the methods of sensory psychophysics have produced an immense amount of reliable and precise information about the different kinds of observation that we make in response to different kinds and degrees of physical stimulation. In Chapter 3, we shall survey psychologists' efforts to analyze the perceived world of objects by psychophysical measures; in a later chapter, we shall examine the attempt to re-assemble these piecemeal observations and JND's into the world we observe. In both of these enterprises, much use has been made of the second class of method, that of analytic introspection, to supplement the procedures of sensory psychophysics.

ANALYTIC INTROSPECTION

The world we face outside of the psychophysical laboratory is not, of course, a simple pure physical event, such as the occurrence of a spot of light or of a single musical note that changes in only one simple way. In order to try to observe the elementary sensations in more normal environments, early sensory psychologists developed a special kind of observation, called *analytic introspection.*

---

* Although Fechner's law that "sensation is proportional to the log of the stimulus measure" is still widely accepted (especially among illumination and acoustical engineers), the results of a recent wide-ranging survey of various sensory qualities by S. S. Stevens and his colleagues suggest a somewhat different relationship. His observers are asked to estimate the apparent magnitudes of different stimuli of varying amounts of physical energy, simply by assigning appropriate numbers to each stimulus. Their estimates generally fit more closely to a power function—say, $S = M^c$—than to Fechner's logarithmic function. The question is still at issue.

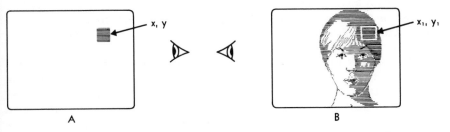

Figure 2-1. The two different procedures intended to discover "sensations": an analogy. (A) Sensory psychophysics, which involves observing a single physical event in isolation—for instance, the single patch marked x, y. (B) Analytic introspection, which is a matter of trying to observe the simple component parts (such as x₁, y₁) of a complex event. An example of this is given in Figure 2-2.

To get some idea of the sense in which this was thought to work, first examine Figure 2-1B. Then look at the cube in Figure 2-2; you normally see it as a light, evenly colored tridimensional object with perpendicular corners and parallel sides. With some effort, however, you can "take it apart" into patches of different lightness, converging edges, and so on. This is a simple form of analytical introspection, in which you have disregarded the "meaning" of the pattern of light and shade. The analytic task is far more

Figure 2-2. Applying analytic introspection to a sample object. To casual observation, the stimulus at (A) appears to be a light-colored cube; that is, it appears to have corners that are right angles, and a surface that is fairly uniformly light on all of its faces. As soon as the point is mentioned, however, you notice that (A) is nothing of the sort. With more careful dissection of the observation, you see that, as at (B) and (C), the angles are very far from being 90°, and the local color grades from dark to light in a very marked manner. This is a particularly easy kind of analytic introspection to undertake since, after all, angle (B) really is an acute angle drawn on paper, and the gradation of ink from one point to the next is quite evident. If you punch three holes in a piece of paper with a pencil point, as shown in (D), and place these holes on (A) so that different regions can be observed in relative isolation, as in (E), you will have performed a primitive form of sensory psychophysics. It was once thought that, with suitable training, one could observe the same "pure sensations" both by means of sensory psychophysics and by analytic introspection. We now know that this is simply not true, as we shall see in Chapter 4.

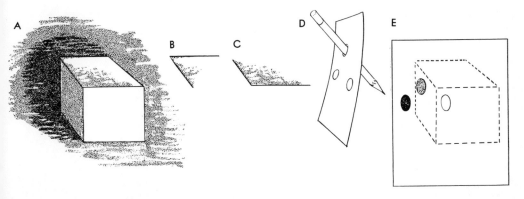

difficult with a real object, such as a box or a table; there, you will need to look at the various parts through a tube or through a hole in a piece of cardboard (as in Figure 2-2D), if you wish to detect the actual change in local color from one region to the next.

Psychologists who considered that all the things we perceive in the world are revealed by careful analytic introspection to be structures or collections of elementary sensations, were called *structuralists*. The central structuralist assumption was this: that, with careful analytic introspection, *the same "pure" sensations could be observed whenever the same stimulus energy falls on the same part of the same sensory organ*. We shall consider some examples of this in a moment. In accordance with this assumption, the myriad of varied objects and events in the world we can observe were thought to be composed of just such elementary sensations in various combinations. In order to understand how we are able to perceive the world, therefore, we would have to understand how we observe the elementary sensations.

Figure 2-3. **A brief outline of the sequence of physical events, essential to perception.** *(A) A distal stimulus object is present (in this case a doorbell). (B) Proximal stimulation reaches the sense organs: 1, light energy; 2, pressure waves in the air ("sound waves"); 3, pressure on the fingertip. (C) The sense organs function to convert proximal stimulation into nerve impulses: 4, eye; 5, ear; 6, tactual receptors in fingertip. (D) The sensory nerves transmit impulses to the brain. (E) The sensory projection areas, where the nerve impulses that originate in the sense organs enter the cerebral cortex (or outer layer) of the brain. Stimulating region 10 causes visual experiences; 11, sounds; 12, touch.*

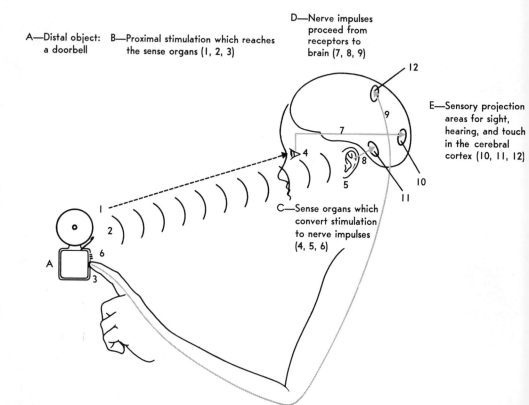

A—Distal object: a doorbell

B—Proximal stimulation which reaches the sense organs (1, 2, 3)

D—Nerve impulses proceed from receptors to brain (7, 8, 9)

E—Sensory projection areas for sight, hearing, and touch in the cerebral cortex (10, 11, 12)

C—Sense organs which convert stimulation to nerve impulses (4, 5, 6)

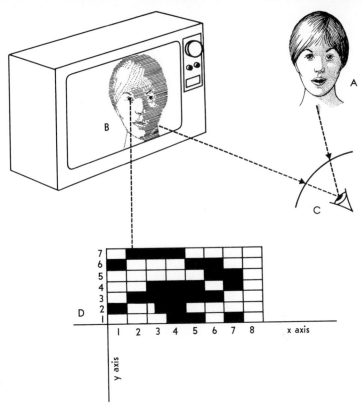

Figure 2-4. How any pattern of proximal stimulation at the eye can be analyzed into simple, elementary physical events. *Any distal object can be duplicated by presenting the appropriate proximal stimulation at each sense organ. For each sense, moreover, we can analyze any complex stimulus distribution into simpler physical events. Thus, the proximal distribution (C) which is produced at the observer's eye by the singer (A) can also be approximated by a TV picture (B). That is, the pattern of light-energy which reaches the eye (C) can be completely analyzed by a system which breaks it down into differences of intensity at different points in space (we temporarily ignore "color"). This is illustrated if we examine closely some portion of the TV picture (D): at x = 2, y = 3, we have a dark* patch (low intensity); at x = 3, y = 1, we have a light patch (high intensity); and, if we hold the paper at arm's length, we see that it all "adds up to" the singer's eye. This same principle is used in any newspaper or magazine photograph, in which, if you look closely, you will see that all forms and shades are built up out of dots of ink of different size and spacing. Other methods of analysis of the stimulation at the eye are equally possible (see pp. 74, 80), but this method will always work.

THE PHYSICAL AND PHYSIOLOGICAL BASES OF OUR SENSATIONS

Structuralists held that each individual sensation is a result of a definite sequence of events, a sequence that could be interfered with at any of several stages (see Figure 2-3), starting, of course, with the physical object.

Distal Objects and Proximal Stimulation

What matters to us in the world is objects and their properties, but our major sensory systems are *not* directly in contact with these objects at all. Therefore, psychologists call them distal stimuli, indicating that they only stimulate our nervous system indirectly, by reflecting light-energy, sound-energy, and so on, which may or may not even reach our sense organs. The energy patterns that do reach and affect our sense organs are called the *proximal stimuli* (Figure 2-4). *We can only know about the distal physical world—the world of space and objects and motion—through these proximal stimulus distributions, acting on our sense organs.* If this pattern of proximal stimulation is interfered with, no object will be observed; conversely, if the proper proximal stimulation can be presented, the object will be observed, even if it is really absent (see Figures 2-3, 2-4). In order to know what proximal distribution will be created by any given distal stimulus object, we need only apply some simple physics (this will be explained in Figure 3-3).

The Elementary Physical Variables.　　　For any given sense modality there is an immense number of proximal stimuli that we may receive. Yet they can all be reduced to, *or reproduced by,* a much smaller number of *elementary physical variables.* Thus, all the events you can see on a TV screen, are reproduced by spots of different brightnesses, at various points on the picture tube (Figure 2-4).

Having analyzed the world of stimulation into elementary physical variables, we must explain how these are translated into nerve action, and then how they are related to the sensations we experience.

Specific Nerve Energies and Projection Areas

For each elementary physical variable, structuralists hoped to find a class of *receptor neuron.* A receptor neuron is a unit of the nervous system sensitive to a particular kind of physical energy.* Thus, there are receptors at the back of the eye which are set into action by light, there are receptors in the skin which respond to pressure, etc. Whenever a receptor neuron is *excited* by stimulating energy, it "fires" and stimulates other neurons deeper in the nervous system, which lead to a special *projection* area on the brain (Figure 2-3E), and from there to the surrounding *association areas.*

Therefore, even when a proximal stimulus is present, if the receptors are prevented from responding to it (say, by anesthetization, or by fatigue), no sensation will occur. And vice versa: Even if no stimuli are present, if we can manage to fire the receptors by other means (or if we can obtain a set of excitations at the appropriate projection area in any other way), the sensation will occur.

If it were possible to hook up the receptor organs from your ear to the projection areas from your eye, and vice versa, you would presumably hear light and see sound. More modestly, applying pressure on the closed eyelid will produce *pressure phosphenes* of faint, purplish light, even though no light has entered your eye. What happens is that the pressure excites receptor neurons back in the retina of the eye, and this excitation, when transmitted to the visual projection area, results in the sensation of light. (Meanwhile in response to the same mechanical force the nerves in the finger and in the eyelid, of course, convey sensations of pressure-touch.) Thus, if the proximal stimulus is missing, we can stimulate the sensory nerves by other means—by

---

* The excitation of such a receptor neuron is called its *specific nerve energy* because it was originally thought that each nerve acted differently from all others; now we know that it is not a question of different nerve action, but rather a question of *where* the impulse from the receptor's neuron enters the cerebral cortex of the brain—that is, the receptor's *projection area.*

electrical or mechanical means, for instance. Similarly, light will be observed if the sensory cortex is itself directly stimulated.

In short, we do not see objects directly, nor do we "see" the retinal image, nor do we "see" the excitation in the optic nerve. At most, we can say that what we "see" is the final effect on the projection area of the cerebral cortex.

"Inside," "Outside," and "Upside Down."   The eye is not like a camera. This is an important point. Remember: The distal stimulus is an object—a songstress, a house, a cloud. This is what we observe. The proximal stimulation is a pattern of high-intensity and low-intensity light-energy at the eye, or a set of atmospheric pressure-waves at the ear, and so on. The nerve activities are still less like the songstress or the house. Rather, they are complicated electrochemical events that can be detected by suitable instruments. The common-sense view of the perceptual process is that somehow the outside object gets inside, and then our minds can examine it. The analogy that the eye is just like a camera, and that our minds examine the upside-down images of the objects on our retinas (or on the sensory projection areas), is only slightly more sophisticated, and equally incorrect.

In fact, there is only one *object,* the songstress, whom we look at and listen to. There is no replica of the object in the brain. Rather, there are characteristic neural processes set up, in the brain, processes that are specific to the songstress, that are different for the house and for the cloud, and that enable us to make different observations about the world.

SUMMARY

Structuralists thought that
for each detectable elementary physical event a specialized receptor neuron (or specific nerve energy) responding to the event could be found and that a corresponding elementary observation (or sensation) would be experienced. Just as we can reduce all possible patterns of proximal stimulation to various combinations of different elementary physical variables, so they hoped to analyze observations into combinations of elementary sensations corresponding to those variables.

A. A slightly changed version of Figure 1-2A appears in Fig. 4-28C3, p. 70. Is the young lady readily observable?

B. The word "concealed" in Figure 1-2B is *word.*

Sensations: The Perception of Elementary Physical Events

The observations of simple physical events are convenient to study because we can vary and measure the stimuli with ease and precision. They also are important because one might hope to build up directly from these *sensations* to an understanding of more complex objects and events. Certainly if the hope were fulfilled, the study of perception would be simplified. In any case, most of our knowledge about our sensory systems was gained in the process of studying such simple physical stimuli.

In this chapter, we shall analyze one sensory system—vision—in some detail, considering the other senses only

3

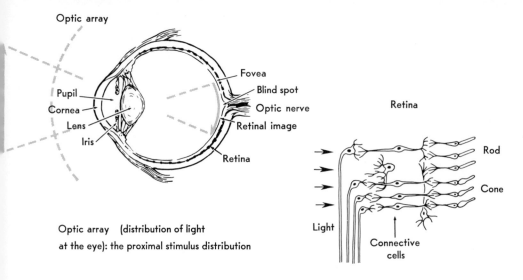

Optic array

Fovea
Pupil
Cornea
Lens
Iris
Blind spot
Optic nerve
Retinal image
Retina

Retina

Rod

Cone

Optic array   (distribution of light
at the eye): the proximal stimulus distribution

Light

Connective
cells

Figure 3-1. *The eye and its major parts. The* lens *is a transparent tissue that focuses light rays, which enter the* cornea, *to form an* image *on the* retina. *The* iris *is a diaphragm of pigmented tissue controlling the size of the* pupil, *thereby regulating the over-all amount of light reaching the retina and compensating for illumination changes. The* retina *is composed of a layer of receptor cells* (rods *and* cones), *which are neurons that are sensitive to light and to changes of light, and a layer of bipolar and ganglion cells. These latter cells are not themselves sensitive to light but are stimulated by interconnected groups of receptor cells. The* fovea *is a small region, central in the retina, that is highly sensitive to detail and consists entirely of cones. The* optic nerve *is the bundle of nerve fibers from the retina of the eye to the projection area in the cortex (via a relay center called the thalamus); it leaves the eye at the* blind spot, *a small region which has no receptors sensitive to light.*

as they happen to contribute to the perception of the world of objects and events in space.

THE VISUAL SENSE: STRUCTURE

The visual system has several parts, of which the eye is only one. The structure of the eye is outlined in Figure 3-1. Within the eye, the retina is the site of visual contact between the world and the nervous system, since that is where light-energy of the optic array is transformed into neural activity. The retinal system includes rods, cones, and connective cells.

The *rods,* which predominate in the periphery of the retina, are very sensitive to light energy and, therefore, are responsible for night vision. They are color blind in the sense that there are no subsets of rods that are specially responsive to one set of wave lengths rather than another. Rods connect to the optic nerve through intertwined connective cells (Figure 3-1), called *bipolar* and *ganglion cells,* which send nerve impulses to the brain from groups of stimulated rods.

The *cones,* of which the *fovea* is composed exclusively, also predominate in different zones in the rest of the central retina. The cones are responsible for color vision, since they are not all equally stimulated by the same wavelengths. Aside from the eye, important related structures are as follows:

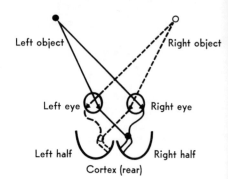

Figure 3-2. Optic pathways. *The outer halves of each retina are connected to the same sides of the brain; the inner halves, to opposite sides of the brain. Note that an object at right affects the left side of the brain, and vice versa.*

1. The *visual projection area* in the brain, to which come the neural impulses from the retina, preserving the general spatial relationships. The visual projection area is not simply a copy of the optic retina, however. The *nasal* (inner) halves of each retina send their impulses by one pathway, the *temporal* (outer) halves by another (Figure 3-2), and we are still not exactly certain about how the contents of the two halves are put together again.

2. From the projection area, neural activity spreads into the *visual association area* in the brain; it becomes very difficult to trace the effects of stimulation systematically any further into the nervous system.

3. *The oculomotor system* is a set of intricately coordinated muscles that move the eyes, permitting them to scan the optic array.

FUNCTION OF THE VISUAL SYSTEM: THE "STATIONARY" EYE

The sensory apparatus of the visual system appears to have evolved for use while in motion, but it is simpler for us to examine it while it is at rest. We shall first analyze the physical characteristics of a single small patch of light, and then consider the ways in which these affect what we see.

Physical Analysis of Stimulation

The pattern of light that confronts the eye is called the *optic array* (A in Figure 3-3). The optic array (and the image on the retina) is found by drawing "rays" to the eye from each point in the object at which an observer is looking. At any such point, the light-energy may vary in the following ways that are known to affect the human eye: in intensity; in predominant wavelength; and in purity, or mixture of wavelengths.

1. *Intensity* is the amount of physical energy present in the light (as measured by the electricity generated in the photocell of a light meter, for example).

Sensations: Perception of Elementary Physical Events

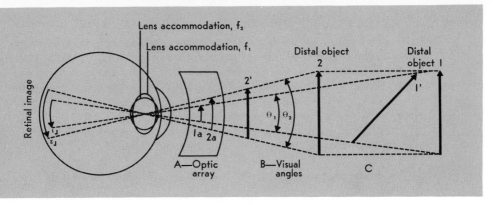

Figure 3-3. *The geometry of vision. To discover what proximal pattern will be produced by any distal object, simple geometry will suffice. Objects (1) and (1') subtend the same visual angle (θ_1), so they project the same optic array and the same retinal images (1a and r₁). Similarly, objects (2) and (2') produce the same visual angle (θ_2), optic array (2a), and retinal image (r_2). However, to bring the retinal image into sharp focus, the curvature of the lens will have to be different for a near object (2') and a far one (2) (that is, the lens will have to* accommodate).

2. *Wavelength* is the distance between the crest of one wave, and the crest of the next, when we consider the wavelike aspects of light-energy (or electromagnetic radiation). Electromagnetic waves range from 1/1,000,000,000 of a millionth of a meter to 100 million meters in length. Of this immense range, only the region between (roughly) 400 and 750 millimicrons,* is observable by the human eye (Figure 3-4B). If, as Isaac Newton showed in 1666, a beam of white-appearing light, such as sunlight, passes through a prism (Figure 3-5A), it will spread out into rays of different wavelengths (and different *hues* will become visible). This is the *spectrum*, and light-energy of any de-

*A *micron* is a millionth of a meter (that is about a millionth of a yard); a *millimicron* is one thousandth of a micron.

Figure 3-4. *The spectrum of electromagnetic radiation. (A) The total range of electromagnetic radiation. (B) The visible spectrum of light-energy (photic radiation).*

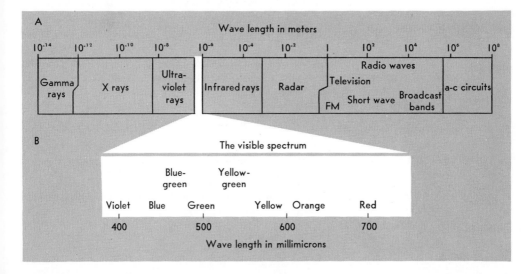

sired wavelength may be obtained by placing a slit at the proper location in a plate, as in Figure 3-5B. It is important to realize that lights of different wavelengths can be mixed and separated indefinitely without affecting one another. When, as we shall see, "red light" and "green light" add together to form "yellow," *the "yellow" is in us, not in the light, which remains unchanged by the mixing* (Figure 3-5C).

3. The *purity* of a light refers to the degree of predominance of one of the wavelengths into which it can be separated by the prism.

What do we see when these physical stimulus attributes are varied?

The Observations of Small Patches of Light:
The Sensations of Color

As we vary a small patch of light-energy, its appearance will normally change in the following simple manner:

1. *Intensity and brightness.* As physical intensity increases, the patch of light appears brighter, as indicated on the vertical axis, A, in Figure 3-6.

2. *Wavelength and hue.* As the wavelength of the patch is varied, the hue of the patch changes from red, through orange, yellow, green, blue, and indigo to violet (B in Figure 3-6).

3. *Purity and saturation.* If a single wavelength of light is used, the hue appears strong and saturated. As other wavelengths are added, it will become diluted, grayer, and less saturated (C in Figure 3-6). Thus, a pure red is more saturated than a pink, even though the two may have the same hue and brightness, whereas a completely desaturated mixture of all of the wavelengths looks gray.

These correlations are by no means perfect,* but the correspondence is quite good as a first approximation. The greatest lack of correspondence occurs between hue and wavelength. Although a given wavelength will normally produce a particular hue for an isolated patch of light (we shall see that this does not hold for complex patterns of light), *it is not true that a particular hue will be observed only with a particular wavelength,* since the same hue can be produced by either a single wavelength, or by a mixture of quite different wavelengths.

The Elements of Color Mixture: The Facts and Theories.　　Let us consider Newton's prismatic experiment (Figure 3-5A) and see why it was not simply an experiment in physics. If we pass white light through a prism, it breaks up into all the colors of the spectrum, and, if we recombine the entire spectrum, we again see white light. If, however, we repeat the experiment, using slits that

*For a given wavelength, the hue and saturation change somewhat with different intensities and, for a given intensity of light, the brightness will change at different wavelengths. Although these changes have been investigated in some detail, they are more relevant to the study of sensory physiology than to perception. If we remember that our central purpose in this chapter is to discover the building blocks of the perceived world, however, a relatively simple story emerges.

will pass only light from three narrow bands of the spectrum—say, 650 (red), 530 (green), and 460 (blue)—we will *also* see white when we combine these three tiny portions of the total spectrum! We have broken down the white light, kept only three colored portions of it, and recombined these to form white again (Figure 3-7A). And, as you might guess, if we can make white by mixing only three wavelengths, *we can match any other color in the spectrum by mixing these three colors, in varying proportions.** We can therefore describe or specify any hue in terms of the proportions of three standard wavelengths (see Figure 3-7B) needed to duplicate it. Although we can experience thousands of different JND's of color, we do not have to consider these to be independent observations, each requiring individual description and exploration. Instead, we can replace this immense catalog of color observations by a much smaller number of elementary color sensations, of which all of the other color observations are composed in various combinations.

Many different triads of wavelengths can duplicate all of the hues. But because these three (Figure 3-7) appear to be relatively "pure" colors, it was believed for many years that they were the primary colors. According to the *Young-Helmholtz theory,*† there are three kinds of cones in the eye, each maximally sensitive to one region of the spectrum (Figure 3-8), and each producing a sensation of one of the primary hues. The three colors were *red, green,* and *blue,* roughly speaking, and all other hues were considered to be combinations of these. This theory, which fits the facts of color-matching with small patches of light very well, was accepted as *the* explanation of color vision for many years, despite the fact that these wavelengths don't appear *really pure* (see Figure 3-10), and despite several other difficulties.

For example, we can observe spots of yellow in zones of the retina where we cannot observe red and green; color deficient observers may be "blind" to red and green, yet not to yellow; and, perhaps most strongly, it seems very hard to accept yellow as being anything but a pure sensation: Violet does look like red and blue, and aqua looks like blue and green, but yellow simply doesn't look like a greenish red.

In fact, if we pay attention to the apparent similarities and differences between hues, as summarized in Figure 3-9, it seems much more appropriate to look for four primary hues, rather than the three primaries shown in Figure 3-8. This is exemplified by the *opponent-colors theory,* proposed in 1955 by psychologists L. Hurvich and D. Jameson, and based on an earlier theory (1872) of physiologist Ewald Hering. It assumes that there are four basic hues (and their corresponding receptor-processes) paired in two sets as explained in Figure 3-10B: a yellow-blue pair and a red-green pair. These two pairs, and a black-white pair, will account neatly for the facts of color mixture, for most color vision defects, and for the appearances of "purity," "similarity," and "dissimilarity" among the hues of the color circle (Figure 3-9). This proposal seems more satisfactory at present than the three-color theory, although the issue is still open.

---

* In fact, we can make some colors that are not in the spectrum at all: The red in the spectrum always looks a little yellowish unless we add some blue; the color purple is completely missing from the spectrum.

† Proposed by Thomas Young in 1845 and developed in its widely accepted form by Hermann von Helmholtz 20 years later.

So far, we have been considering the different colors of a single patch of light; in addition, patches may differ in their location in the optic array, and, if we could not distinguish one place from another, we could make little use of our eyes other than to tell night from day. We shall break this problem into two parts: *acuity,* or the ability to detect a separation between two points; and *local sign,* or direction-sensitivity.

The Importance, Measures, and Conditions of Acuity

In order for us to tell one object, one facial expression, or one letter from another, *some* specific, different receptor activities must be stimulated. We *might,* conceivably, have receptors sensitive to smiles vs. frowns, a's vs. b's, circles vs. squares. This is both unlikely and uneconomical, however. Let's see what the most economical arrangement would be like.

What is the simplest system that could make all these discriminations? A *mosaic* of retinal receptors, as in Figure 3-11, each element of which sends

Figure 3-5. The independence of wavelengths and the integration of hues. *(A) A beam of white-appearing light-energy will spread out into a spectrum whose appearance varies from violet at the short-wavelength end to red at the long-wavelength end. If we select two narrow beams of light from this spectrum by placing two slits in a solid plate, as shown at (B), those beams can be recombined to fall on a single spot, and the hues will then "mix" into a new hue; thus, a red-appearing beam and a green-appearing beam produce a yellow-appearing spot. The wavelengths of light-energy themselves do not mix, however, since the combined beam can be redivided by passing it through a prism (C) into the two original beams, whereas a yellow-appearing beam taken from the spectrum at (B) would pass unchanged through a second prism.*

Figure 3-6. The distinguishable sensations of color. *Patches of color may differ from each other in brightness (A), hue (B), and saturation (C), which is the dimension that runs from gray (or "colorless") to fully colored. About 350,000 JND's can be distinguished.*

Figure 3-7. The facts of trichromatic color mixture. *Three beams of light taken from different regions of the spectrum will, when mixed in the proper proportions, produce the hues of the entire spectrum, including white. At (A), we see how they will combine to form white. At (B), we see the proportions of each of reddish-, greenish-, and bluish-appearing light-energy needed to match the appearance of any point on the spectrum, which is laid out on the horizontal axis. Thus, to match 580 millimicrons (yellow light), take about equal parts of 650 and 530 (reddish and greenish light, respectively). Note that you can't tell simply by looking at the curve in this diagram what perceived hue will be produced by each mixture (that is, 580 is yellow, not a reddish-green); rather, you have to look down at the labels on the horizontal axis to find out.*

Sensations:
Perception
of Elementary
Physical
Events

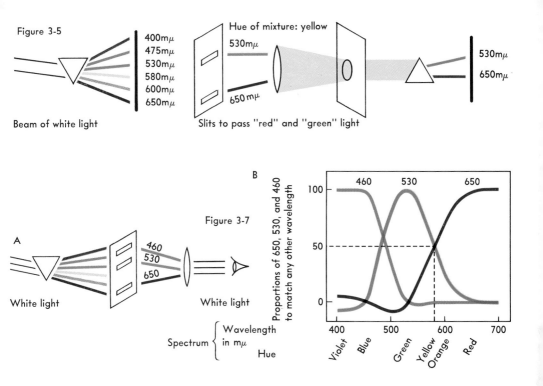

Figure 3-5

400mμ
475mμ
530mμ
580mμ
600mμ
650mμ

Beam of white light

Hue of mixture: yellow

530mμ

650mμ

Slits to pass "red" and "green" light

530mμ

650mμ

B

Figure 3-7

Proportions of 650, 530, and 460 to match any other wavelength

460   530   650

100

50

0

400   500   600   700

Violet Blue Green Yellow Orange Red

A

460
530
650

White light

White light

Spectrum { Wavelength in mμ / Hue

Figure 3-6

B: JND's of hue

C: JND's of saturation

JND's of brightness

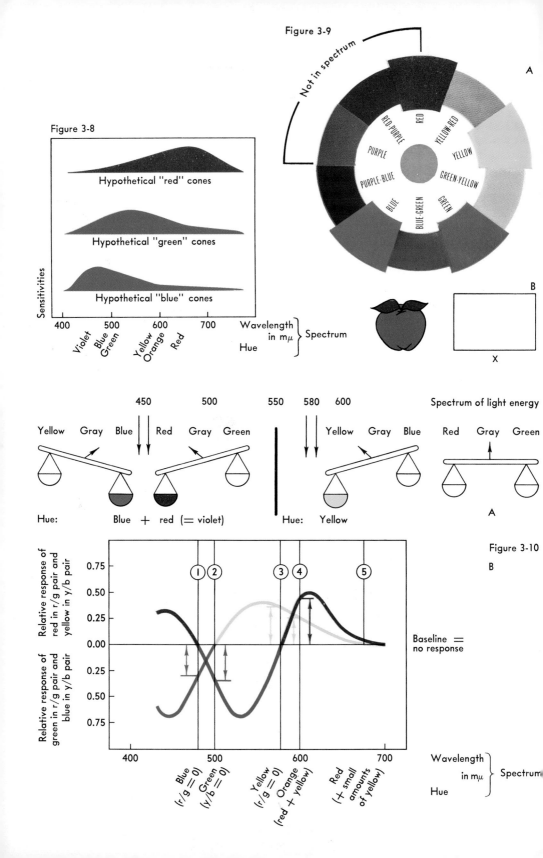

Figure 3-9

Not in spectrum

RED-PURPLE · RED · YELLOW-RED
PURPLE · · YELLOW
PURPLE-BLUE · · GREEN-YELLOW
BLUE · BLUE-GREEN · GREEN

A

B

X

Figure 3-8

Hypothetical "red" cones

Hypothetical "green" cones

Hypothetical "blue" cones

Sensitivities

400   500   600   700   Wavelength in mμ ⎫ Spectrum
Violet Blue Yellow Red   ⎬
       Green Orange   Hue   ⎭

450   500   550 580 600   Spectrum of light energy

Yellow Gray Blue   Red Gray Green   Yellow Gray Blue   Red Gray Green

Hue: Blue + red (= violet)   Hue: Yellow   A

Figure 3-10

B

Relative response of red in r/g pair and yellow in y/b pair

0.75
0.50
0.25
0.00
0.25
0.50
0.75

Relative response of green in r/g pair and blue in y/b pair

① ②   ③ ④   ⑤

Baseline = no response

400   500   600   700   Wavelength in mμ ⎫ Spectrum
                                                                          ⎬
Blue   Green   Yellow Orange   Red   Hue   ⎭
(r/g = 0)(y/b = 0)(r/g = 0)(red + (+ small
                          yellow) amounts
                                   of yellow)

Figure 3-8. The Young-Helmholtz theory of color sensitivity. The simplest way in which to account for the color-mixture facts outlined in Figure 3-7 is to assume that there are three different kinds of receptors: cones maximally sensitive to 650 millimicrons, which when stimulated alone produce the sensation of red; cones maximally sensitive to 530 millimicrons ("green"); and cones maximally sensitive to 460 millimicrons ("blue").

Figure 3-9. The color circle: complementaries, adaptation, and after-images. (A) Without referring to wavelengths at all, we can summarize color phenomena as follows. There are four unique hues (red, yellow, green, and blue) that do not resemble one another; equal quantities of complementaries (hues that are on opposite sides of the circle) yield gray when they are mixed; unequal proportions of complementaries yield the color of the predominant component, but with a lower saturation. (B) If you stare at any colored patch—say, the apple in (B)— for some time, adaptation, or fatigue, will occur, and the color will become gradually less saturated. Next, look at an illuminated surface of neutral color (as in X). An after-image of the first patch will be seen, but it will be of complementary color.

Figure 3-10. The opponent-colors theory (Hurvich and Jameson). Assume that all hue sensations are produced by two pairs of receptors, one pair (r/g) producing either red or green sensation and a second pair (y/b) producing either yellow or blue. The two members in each pair are opponents: We cannot experience a yellowish blue or a reddish green. If both members of a single pair are equally stimulated, they cancel each other, leaving only gray; if one member is stimulated more than its opponent, its hue will be seen. Thus, the spectrum at 450 mμ stimulates both pairs of receptors and looks reddish blue (violet), while 580 mμ stimulates only the y/b pair and looks yellow (A). All the hues that we can see are therefore either reddish yellows, reddish blues, greenish yellows, or greenish blues, and in order to predict exactly what hue will be seen with any given mixture of light, we must know the sensitivity of each receptor pair to the wavelengths of the spectrum.

How can the sensitivity curves of these receptor pairs be determined? The amount of the blue response at 450 mμ is measured by adding just enough light that is pure yellow in appearance (about 580 mμ) to cancel the blue. Similarly, the amount of yellow response at each wavelength in the yellowish regions of the spectrum is measured by adding just enough pure blue to cancel the yellow; pure red is used to measure the green response in the greenish regions of the spectrum, and pure green, to measure the red response.

The graph at B shows the amount of yellow or blue response and of red or green response that is produced at each wavelength, measured in this manner. Unlike the Young-Helmholtz sensitivity curves (in Figure 3-8), this graph tells us what hue will be seen at any given wavelength. Thus, at point (4), red plus yellow = yellowish red (that is, orange); at point (1) (475 mμ), r/g = 0, leaving pure blue; at (2) (500 mμ), y/b = 0, leaving pure green; at (3) (580 mμ), r/g = 0 again, leaving pure yellow. Notice that yellow is present throughout the long wavelengths, (5). This is why a "red" of 650 and a "green" of 530 mix to give yellow: because light at 650 mμ stimulates both red and yellow responses, light at 530 mμ stimulates both green and yellow responses, and only the yellow remains after the red and green cancel each other (not because yellow is composed of red and green sensations, as the Young-Helmholtz theory asserts).

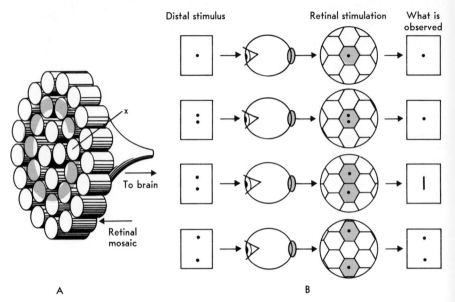

Distal stimulus   Retinal stimulation   What is observed

A

B

Figure 3-11. **The mosaic model of acuity.** *(A) Unless the gap in the letter C is large enough to leave one receptor, x, unstimulated, the C should be indistinguishable from an O. (B) Similarly, only if an intervening receptor remains unstimulated, would we expect two points to be distinguishable from one (after Asher).*

Figure 3-12. **Diagnostic tests of visual acuity.** *These are usually eye charts—for example, letters, as in the Snellen chart, or E's facing in different directions—in which a subject must see a gap between parts of the figure in order to respond correctly. (A) Normal vision. (B) Myopia: Near objects are focused readily; concave lenses needed for far objects. (C) Hypermetropia: Far objects are focused readily; convex lenses needed for near objects (reading). (D) Presbyopia: Loss of ability to focus near objects as age increases (see table).*

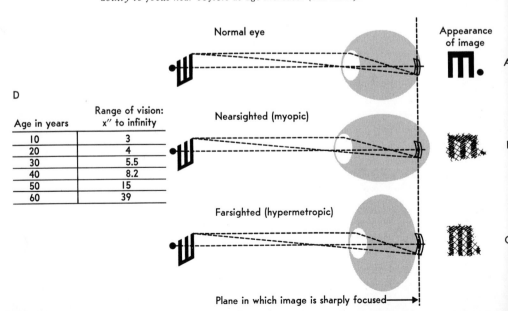

Normal eye   Appearance of image

D

Age in years	Range of vision: x″ to infinity
10	3
20	4
30	5.5
40	8.2
50	15
60	39

Nearsighted (myopic)

Farsighted (hypermetropic)

Plane in which image is sharply focused⟶

a single message to some separate place in the brain, would do. How could such a system distinguish the letter *C* from an *O*, for example? By the fact that the gap in the *C* leaves one receptor unstimulated. If in A the gap in the letter "C" were too small, we would see a circle instead; if the dots at B were too close, we would see a single point. The ability to distinguish such fine separation is called *acuity*. It is essentially a JND of separation, and it has two general measures, *diagnostic* and *research*.

Diagnostic Tests. The lens of the eye changes shape, or accommodates, in order to bring objects at different distances to the same focus on the retina (this was shown in Figure 3-3). More than 25 per cent of the population are unable to focus equally well at all distances (see Figure 3-12). Since such defects are usually correctable, standardized acuity tests have been devised. Either the size of the gap which must be detected is varied from one line to the next on the chart, or the size of the retinal image is varied by having the subject approach until he can just make it out.*

Research Measure: Visual Angle. For most scientific and technical purposes, the *visual angle subtended at the eye* is used to measure the size of a proximal stimulus because, regardless of distance, the retinal image's size remains constant for a given visual angle (see Figure 3-3). In general, a separation between two points that subtends an angle of at least 1/60th of a degree at the eye will be detected as a separation.

The Distribution of Acuity over the Retina. Only in the foveal region of the retinal image can details be made out. As we depart from the central fovea, visual acuity deteriorates alarmingly; by $5°$, it has dropped 50 per cent (Figure 3-13B). Moreover, *the eye is completely blind* where the optic nerve leaves the eye (see Figures 3-1 and 3-14).

Why have you never noticed it before?

Firstly, we do not see the *blind spot* because what the blind spot in one eye misses, the other eye picks up. Secondly, there is no black spot in the world that we can observe, even with one eye alone: Things tend to complete themselves, when interrupted by the blind spot (Figure 3-14), and a line that falls across that spot is not seen as any shorter than when it falls elsewhere. Such filling-in processes are quite general in perception, but only a bare beginning has been made at research into this quite fascinating phenomenon. Most importantly, the blind spot is far from the fovea, and we normally scan the world around us by probing around with our sensitive foveas, much as you might cast about with a flashlight in the dark. Normal vision is not stationary vision.

---

* Thus, by the first measure, if the average person can read the fourth line at 20 feet, and so can you, your acuity is a normal 20/20; by the second procedure, the number of feet from which you can read what the normal person can read at 20 feet is the measure of your acuity, and the higher the score, the greater the acuity. Acuity defects differ in the effect of distance (see Figure 3-12) so that vision tests should fit the tasks for which people are being selected.

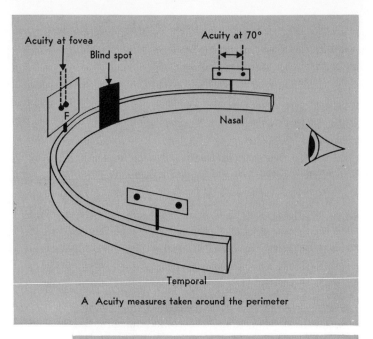

A Acuity measures taken around the perimeter

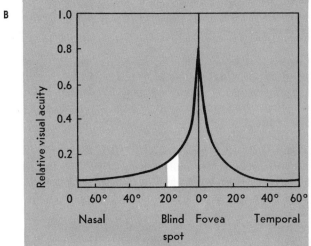

Figure 3-13. **The surprising narrowness of the momentary gaze.** *(A) A perimetry experiment to measure acuity at various distances from the fovea. The observer is looking straight at the fixation point (F). Note the wider separation needed to detect the separation between the test dots at the sides. (B) The percentages of acuity at different distances from the fovea.*

Figure 3-14. **The blind spot.** *Close your left eye and fixate the X with your right eye. Adjust your distance from the page until the white disc at right disappears on the blind-spot of your eye. See Figure 3-13A for further details. Is there an evident interruption of the checkerboard pattern when the white disc disappears?*

It is not enough to be able
to detect whether two patches are separated in space; we have to perceive
where they are in relationship to each other if our perceptual systems are
to rebuild our perceived world out of these bits and pieces into which
psychologists and physiologists have been analyzing it.

Consider points *A*, *B*, and *C*, below. Do we simply see three separated

$$C.$$

$$A \quad B \quad D$$

points or are *B* and *C* in different *directions* from the center, *A*? A fourth
point, *D*, is not simply one more point. It is in line with *A* and *B*, and the
four points constitute a distinct spatial pattern, or *shape*. Each point seems
to carry some sensation of location—a *local sign*—in addition to sensations of
color. For a long time, it was thought that no local signs exist at birth, but
that they are supplied by eye-movements, and that the brain registers that
one has to move the eye *down* from *C* to *A*, and to the *right*, from *A* to *D*.
However, because of the ability to discern shapes with *exposures too short
for any eye-movements to be made* (less than 0.2 seconds), this hypothesis
has been discarded.

This is not to say, however, that eye-movements do not contribute to the
observation of where things are located. As we shall now see, eye-movements
are overwhelmingly important to this ability.

THE MOVING EYE: EYE-MOVEMENTS AND REFLEXES

For a stationary eye and a stationary observer, the position of any point
out in space is simply projected to some point on the retina and on the cortex
(Figure 2-3 and 3-1). Given the position of the point on the retina, we know
its direction in space.

This stationary case is not at all usual, however. The observer's body is in
almost constant motion in the world, his head is in motion on his trunk, and
his eyes are in motion in his head. Two kinds of eye movement are essential
for the perception of moving objects by moving observers in a three-dimensional world. *Compensatory movements* permit the eye to fix some target while
the body moves (Figure 3-15A), and *pursuit movements* swing the eyes
smoothly to obtain clear foveal images from moving objects. Further,
accommodation and convergence bring the object to which we are attending
into clear focus and central location on the retina (Figure 3-15B). Normal
vision would be quite impossible without the cooperation of all of these
muscular actions, and they must all be taken into account in some fashion
in order to assign any spatial meaning to a given stimulation of the retina.
In order to know where the distal object is in space we have to know how
our eye has been moved. Only then could we interpret the image on the

Sensations:
Perception
of Elementary
Physical
Events

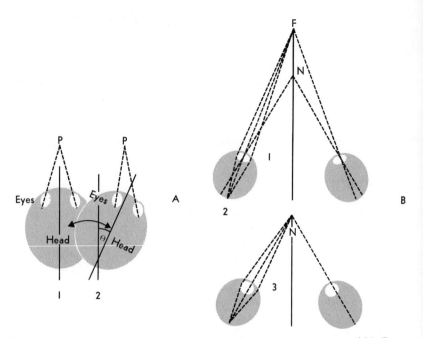

Figure 3-15. **Compensatory movements, accommodation, and convergence.** *(A) Compensatory motions are smoothly and precisely executed. Fixate some point (P), straight ahead (1); keeping your gaze fixed on (P), rotate your head from side to side. Do your eyes seem to be moving? The drawing shows the closely coordinated motions this task actually demands. If you repeat this action, but nod your head vertically as you shake it from side to side and also move your torso a little (in addition, the fixation point may be moving in space!), you will still be able to maintain fixation accurately and effortlessly—but we couldn't begin to draw the kinds of complex compensatory movements needed to do this. (B) Accommodation and convergence are used in fixating points at different distances. As a point to which we are attending approaches the eyes from far (F) to near, (N), the shape of the lens changes (1 to 3) to keep the focus clearly on the retina (2). This is* accommodation. *Coordinated with this, the angle between the eyes changes, to bring the point on to the fovea of each eye. This is* convergence.

retina (Figure 3-16). Consider this example. Move your eye smoothly from point *A* to point *B* below; the page remains stationary. If, however, you

A.   B.

produce the same change in retinal image by fixating point *B* and then moving your eyeball back and forth by pressing at the side of the upper eyelid, the page appears to move in space as the retinal image moves across the eye. What is different in the way one and the same motion of the retinal image was obtained in the two situations?

Unless some form of correction were made continually for our unceasing eye-movement, shapes would dissolve into kaleidoscopic chaos, since the eye

Figure 3-16. **The spatial meaning of a local sign depends on knowing the position of the eye itself.** *The relationship between the movable eye and the fixed brain may be illustrated by the analogy of a fixed TV receiver on which is displayed the image picked up by a moving TV camera. The location of any point in space cannot be determined from the location of its image in the receiver alone, since it also depends on the position of the camera. We might know the position of the camera by receiving information about how it is tilted or raised (mechanisms 1, 2), as in (B) and (C). Analogously in the case of the eye, there might be sensations from kinesthetic receptors in the eye muscles that tell us which way the muscles are pulling the eye. We might also know about the camera's position by having the script (3) that the camera is following. In the case of the eye, this would mean that the brain would have to keep track of the orders that are sent to the eye muscles. The relative contributions of these sources of information is still at issue, and we shall see in Chapter 5 that there are still other means by which the motion of the eye might be detected and "taken into account."*

searches the world without stopping, bringing various points of interest into the clear spotlight of the fovea. There are several ways in which we could get information (or *feedback*) about how our eye has been moved, and the relative importance of their contributions is still undecided (Figure 3-16).

This is a good place to stop and survey how much of the perceived world we can now explain—since we have, in fact, obtained all of the necessary analytic elements if the simplest structuralist assumptions are correct.

THE SENSE OF SIGHT: SUMMARY AND PREVIEW

The objects and events of the world we see affect our sensory system only indirectly, through the optic array, or pattern of proximal stimulation, of light reaching the eye. If we consider a small homogeneous patch of light-energy at any point in the optic array, that patch can be completely specified in terms of its wavelength mixture, its intensity, and its position in the array. (This *must* be possible in *every* case; we shall see later, however, that there may be much better ways in which to analyze and discuss the optic array.)

With each change in the physical variables of predominant wavelength, wavelength balance, and intensity of such a homogeneous patch of light, normal human beings observe changes of hue, saturation, and brightness.

Thus, for a small patch taken *from any scene at all*, we can predict its sensation (that is, its appearance in isolation) simply from those physical measures. The intensities of light-energy at, say, 460, 530, and 650 mμ in wavelength, and two spatial coordinates needed to locate the point in two dimensions—these five measures, taken together, will permit us to specify or duplicate the appearance of any point. In one sense, our analysis of the process of visual observation is completed.

If we do stop here, however, almost all our normal observations of the world go unexplained. How does a near object differ from a far one? How does a smile differ from a frown? How do we perceive the infinite variety of nature and the subtleties of our civilized surroundings?

In short, how can we put together the world of perceived things and people out of the observations of spots and patches, which is all we have studied up to this point?

The first solution (which we shall consider briefly in the first part of the next chapter) was simply to add the sensations together—and, it must be admitted, for certain kinds of observations, this appears to work quite well. The perception of a near object might differ from that of a far one, because of the tactual-kinesthetic sensations which are caused by the differences in convergence needed to fixate them (Figure 3-15). A smile may differ from a frown, in that the local signs of the individual sensations that "compose" the smile follow an upward curve, whereas those for a frown follow a downward curve, and we have learned to expect different interpersonal consequences for the two different aggregations of sensation.

In the next chapter, then, we shall attempt to put the pieces together. Instead of the perception of individual patches in a two-dimensional plane, and the contributions of only one sensory system, we shall consider the perception of solid objects in tridimensional space.

Perceiving Objects as Structures of Sensations

In some situations the findings of sensory psychophysics may be applied directly. How much light-energy is needed for a lighthouse beacon to be seen from ten miles away on a dark night? How high in frequency must a hi-fi set go in order to reproduce all the sounds we can hear?

Most objects are vastly more complicated, however. How can we study these? The structuralists' simple assumption was, as we have seen, that the sensations (the observations of simple, isolated physical stimuli under the controlled conditions of sensory psychophysics) are still experienced even when the simple physical stimuli are

4

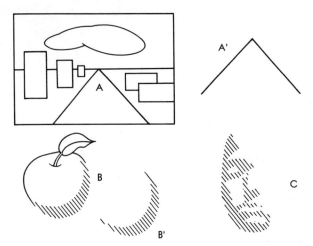

Figure 4-1. The world of "raw experience." The landscape scene at (A) can, with careful analysis, be seen to consist only of two-dimensional arrangements of lines: For example, the "road" is really only two lines which form the angle (A'). What are the "raw experiences" produced by (B) and (C)? See Figure 2-2 for another example. Now, look up from the page and, with one eye closed and your head stationary, inspect the room in front of you. With some effort, you will be able to see the room as a flat, disjointed arrangement of light, shade, and colors. To the extent that you are successful, you will have succeeded in taking the first step in the procedures of analytical introspection. This analytical procedure can be applied to your other senses as well. Consider a completely familiar word— say, "mother." It carries a host of meanings, memories, attitudes, and feelings. Now, repeat it aloud several times, while trying to listen to the sounds alone. With some effort and repetition, you may be able to hear those sounds without meaning—as though they were in some unknown language.

embedded in more complex stimuli, and that they can then be studied by the careful kind of observation called analytic introspection.

STRUCTURALIST CONCEPTS AND METHODS

In some cases, analytic introspection of the world around us does indeed appear to reveal the component sensations—if we dissect our observations carefully enough (see Figure 4-1). Observers had to be trained to separate their "raw sensations" from their knowledge and memories about what the stimulus object is really like.

The justification of this method depends, of course, upon the success with which one can in this way really uncover true elements, which presumably are the same for all men; * otherwise, the method is fruitless.

Perceptions: Sensations plus Memory Images

In line with what we have just said, the structuralists thought the world of perception is composed of *two* kinds of elements:

* This method excludes most observers. We cannot study the insane, those too young to cooperate, or animals. Would this limit psychology too strenuously? Not by the terms of the structuralist assumptions. Since the sensations of all men would be the same, the complete cataloging and study of the sensations would, when finished, be just as applicable to the very young child as to the learned scientist who had undertaken their observation. After all, there are many kinds of scientific observations that require long preparation, apparatus and training, and the structuralists felt that there is no reason to expect the psychology of perception to be an exception.

1. *Sensations,* which we observe when each individual receptor is stimulated.

2. *Memory images,* which are the recollections of previous sensations.

Sensations were discussed in Chapter 3. As for memory images, they were presumed to be dimmer than, but otherwise similar to, the sensations whose "traces," or after-effects, they are (Figure 4-2). How do they occur when there are no proximal stimuli present at the sense organs? There is a very old theory about this: *If two sensations occur together a number of times, and if one sensation (or memory image) should occur alone, then the memory image of the other sensation will also occur.** Thus, if sensations of hammer impact and loud noise have occurred frequently together (or lip movements and sound of the words, and so on), the sight of the hammer alone will cause the bang to be experienced.†

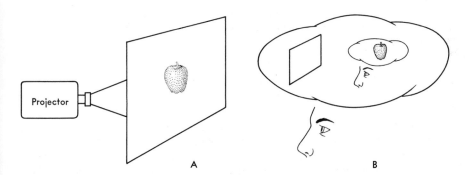

Projector

A   B

Figure 4-2. Mistaking "images" for "sensations." Images and sensations seem to differ from each other in degree, not in kind, according to an important experiment performed in 1910 (and never repeated since). If you were instructed to imagine an apple being displayed on a screen, and a real but dim picture were actually projected on that screen, as in (A), you would probably not detect the picture as being real. Instead, even though (A) would be visible as a picture to any bystander, you would mistake it for an imagined apple (B) (Perky).

With these two sets of components, sensations and images, we should be able to account for all the things and happenings we can observe, if we knew the rules by which the components combine.

What might the structuralist laws of combination be? Most simply, sensations might just add together, and the observation of a group of simple stimuli

* Do not confuse the *retinal image,* which is the pattern of light-energy on the retina, with the *memory image,* whose existence is considerably more difficult to establish.

† This doctrine has at least 200 years of continuous tradition (in fact, statements of it appear in the fifth century B.C.), and it appears frequently in textbooks as "scientific fact." Yet it stands today without one shred of reliable direct evidence to support it; with considerable indirect evidence to circumscribe its validity (p. 61); and with a sheer weight of inapplicability (pp. 62, 67) that makes its continued promulgation as fact, today, incomprehensible.

might simply consist of the *sum* of all the sensations that would have occurred if each stimulus had been presented separately, plus the images that have been associated with them. We shall call this the *addition hypothesis.**

The Special Importance of Space

By the structuralist assumptions, all we see is composed of JND's of light and shade, points or patches of color. *We have no receptors for "motion," "approach," "causation"; we have no receptors for "anger," "cuteness," "sexual attractiveness."* How can we perceive these qualities and events?

We may not have to explain how we perceive each and every possible event, however, since *all* possible events take place in space and time. Once we have explained the perception of objects in space, have we not explained the perception of all things we can observe? Isn't the perception of an object's movement explained if we understand how we see the object at different points in space at each moment in time and put the whole sequence of images together in our memory?

The primary problem, then, was to discover how our visual sensations combine with the images acquired in our past experiences, in order to construct our perceptions of space and spatial position.

THE PERCEPTION OF TWO-DIMENSIONAL SHAPES AND SOLID OBJECTS AT A DISTANCE

The study of space perception had two early sources (although other reasons for interest have appeared since then): (1) the practical, technical problems of depth representation—that is, how to make man see spatial distance where there really isn't any; (2) philosophical questions about how (or whether) man can know the physical world.

The first task is epitomized by Leonardo da Vinci's penetrating analysis of spatial representation in the sixteenth century, and many of his observations of the world of vision and his prescriptions to artists about how to portray it are now listed in our psychology textbooks as the *monocular depth cues*. The second task is represented by Bishop Berkeley's *New Theory of Vision*, which was written in the eighteenth century to prove a philosophical point and which elaborated a detailed and tremendously influential psychological theory in the process of doing so. Both of these sources have left their marks on present problems and prejudices.

The Portrayal of Depth and Distance: The Depth Cues

A *depth cue* (or clue) is a pattern of proximal stimulation that can convey information about the spatial locations of distal objects. The *monocular depth* cues convey information

* It is frequently called the "constancy hypothesis" (K. Koffka. *Principles of Gestalt psychology*. New York: Harcourt, Brace, 1935), because a *constant* relationship is assumed to hold between the parts of the proximal stimulus pattern and the experience that results from them, regardless of what else is happening in the optic array and in the nervous system.

Figure 4-3. **The monocular depth cues as prescriptions for painters.** *(A) Side view of scene. The means of portraying tridimensional space on flat canvas were dis-covered by tracing the view on a "picture plane" of glass (P) held between the eye and the scene. Examining the tracings on the picture plane shows the cues that should be employed by the painter; some of these are listed below and are dis-played at (B). (B) Front view of scene. (C) A demonstration of the cue of illumination (see explanation below).*

List of monocular depth cues: *(W) Interposition.* Notice that rectangle 4 interrupts the outline of 5; this is a strong and effective depth cue, but it only indi-cates which of the objects is in front, not how much distance there is between them. *(X) Linear and size perspective.* Although lines 7–9, 6–8 are parallel on the ground, their tracings converge in the picture plane; similarly, 6–8–9–7 is a trapezoid on the picture plane, though it depicts a rectangle on the ground. Fol-lowing the same geometry, the same-sized boy (1, 2) and the same-sized rectangles (4, 5) produce smaller tracings when they are at greater distances: this is called size perspective, or the cue of relative size. Both of these sets of cues are ef-fective. *(Y) Familiar size.* We know that the man (3), must be physically taller than the boy (1) yet they produce images of the same size; therefore, knowing their true sizes, we might deduce on the basis of their tracing sizes (B1, 3) that the man is more distant than the boy. This is a weak or ineffective cue (see Figures 5-3 to 5-5). *(Z) Illumination direction.* Cover the right half of the picture in (C): which corner looks nearer, 1 or 2? Now cover the left half: which looks nearer, 3 or 4? Uncover both halves. What was responsible for the differences between 1 and 2, 3 and 4?

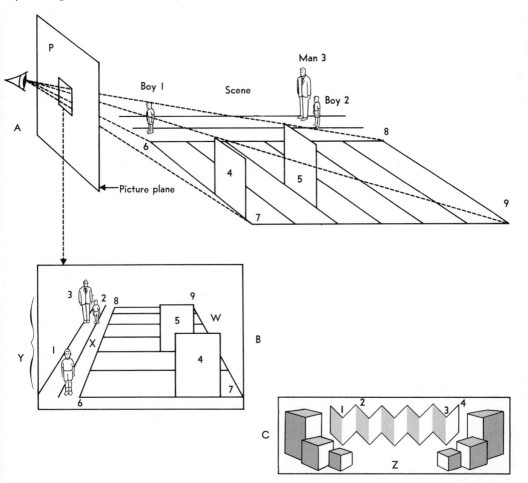

about space by the use of one eye alone; the *binocular* cues depend on the two eyes for their use. The principal traditional monocular visual cues are interposition, linear and size perspective, familiar size, the distribution of shadows and illumination (see the descriptions in Figure 4-3). What makes them important to psychologists?

Pictures as Surrogates for Other Distal Objects.   First let us see why they are important to artists. When an artist wants to draw a recognizable scene— say, a landscape—his intention is roughly as follows (although he does not phrase it this way): *to create a stimulus object to which people will respond in much the same way as they would have responded to the countryside itself.* That is, he intends to produce a *surrogate* of the countryside. He obviously cannot do this in its entirety. He cannot produce a surrogate with real bark, real trees, real clouds moving in real distance, so he must *abstract* only those aspects that are *necessary* to obtain the desired effect yet are reproducible by pigment spread on a flat surface of canvas or paper.

Like the artist's canvas, the retinas of our eyes are essentially flat. It seems reasonable now, as it did centuries ago, to believe that those *patterns* of pigment on a surface that cause us to perceive depth when we look at a picture tell us something about what must fall on the retinas of our eyes if we are to perceive distance and solidity when we look at the real objects in the real world around us. A number of these clues to what the three-dimensional arrangement might be are listed and explained in the caption for Figure 4-3. This list is quite traditional. These depth cues have appeared in many texts for artists, for opticians, and for psychologists, through the centuries, as the causes of the illusion of space in pictures, and of the perception of space in reality. These cues are the patterns that are likely to occur in the *picture plane* (Figure 4-3B) and in the proximal stimulation at the eye when objects are viewed from different distances. Thus, each cue, by *definition*, is a two-dimensional picture of some three-dimensional arrangement. Therefore, each cue must be ambiguous in the sense that the same retinal image could be produced either by a two-dimensional pattern or by some three-dimensional arrangement, and *any theory that bases our perception of space on these depth cues must consider space-perception itself to be equally ambiguous.*

Each pictorial cue produces an optic array that is shared by every member of an entire family of different three-dimensional arrangements (obtained by changing the value of the three-dimensional distance, for each point in the picture plane A, as shown in Figure 4-4A). Exactly the same reasoning applies to the observation of any *individual* point we consider in the retinal image; although its local sign will fix its observed position in two dimensions, P′, the very same point could be stimulated by an object at *any* distance from the eye: $P_1, P_2 \cdots P_n$ (Figure 4-4B).

This is a classical argument, which has been repeated ever since Berkeley presented it in 1709. Thus, as long as we consider our perceptions of objects to be composed of sensations, each of which corresponds to some *point* in the proximal stimulation, we must conclude that *we cannot see the distance of any object by means of vision alone.* We must, if we are to preserve the structuralist attempt, seek the explanation for visual space-perception elsewhere than in *monocular* visual stimulation.

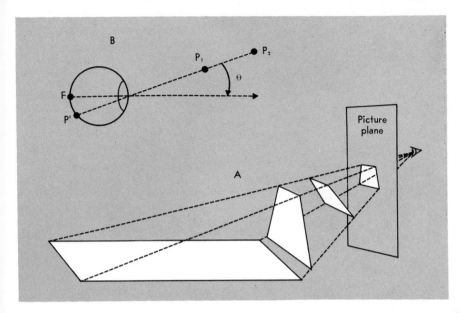

Figure 4-4. The ambiguity of a stationary monocular retinal image. (A) Since the proximal stimulus pattern for the eye is two-dimensional, an infinite number of different tridimensional spatial arrangements will produce the same pattern at the eye. (B) If we consider any light-sensitive point on the retina (P'), it would respond in exactly the same way whether the distal stimulus is at distance P_1, P_2, etc.

Informativeness and Limitations of Binocular Visual Depth Cues. Our two eyes view the world from slightly different positions, so that there is in general a difference, or *disparity,* between the images they receive (Figure 4-5B). Since the binocular disparity our eyes normally receive is a function of the spatial arrangements in the world we regard, it is not surprising that this disparity in itself can be a powerful depth cue. If we take two photographs of a scene, one from the position of each eye (that is, from about 65 mm apart), and then present each picture to its appropriate eye, a remarkably strong spatial effect will be obtained. Devices for viewing such disparate pictures are called stereoscopes. A particularly simple procedure is described in Figure 4-5B, which, if followed, will produce depth effects with the stereograms of Figure 4-6 (pp. 40–41).*

The cue of binocular disparity has been considered as a primary indication of depth more frequently than any other. Unlike convergence and accomodation (pp. 28, 43) it is visual; unlike the other static visual depth cues, there seems to be a clear and necessary connection between the spatial distance of a point and the stereoscopic disparity between the retinal images of the point (Figure 4-7, p. 42). It is not too hard to imagine complex physiologi-

* Not all observers exhibit such stereoscopic vision, since some imbalance between the two eyes may lead to inhibition of the information from one of them.

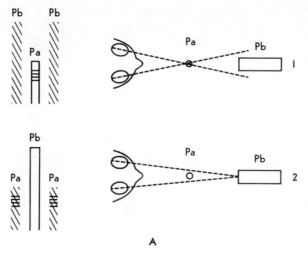

Figure 4-5. **The binocular visual depth cues.** *Because the two eyes see the three-dimensional world from slightly different positions, the view each eye receives is somewhat different. Differences in these views provide two kinds of depth cues: double images and binocular disparity. Neither of these can be produced and used in pictures without special devices, and their absence contributes to the "flatness" of ordinary pictures.*

(A) **Double images**
Hold a pencil (Pa) vertically about one foot straight ahead, lined up

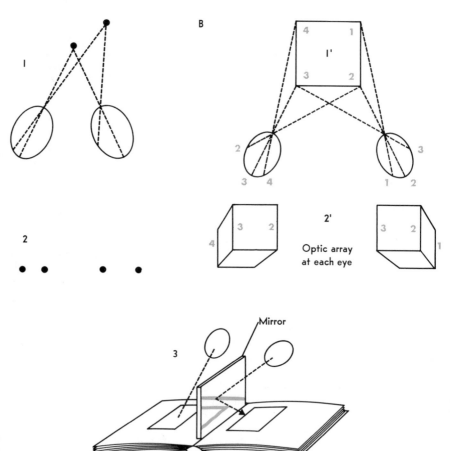

Optic array at each eye

with some vertical edge on a more distant wall (Pb). Fixate Pa (as at 1) and examine Pb carefully: It appears doubled, and you cannot tell, without closing one eye, which contributes which image. When you fixate Pb, double images of the pencil (Pa) appear. Double images can, with great effort, be observed to fill the world as viewed with two eyes, shifting and swirling with each change of fixation. Add the confusion of double-images to that caused by eye-movements, and the uselessness of the camera analogies (p. 15) becomes most evident.

(B) Binocular disparity. Each eye receives a different view of any near three-dimensional arrangement. At (1) and (1'), a schematic diagram illustrates the basis of the disparity, and at (2) and (2') what you would see with each eye separately. (Remember that the retinal image in each eye is reversed and inverted, if you find the diagram confusing.) This depth cue was discovered in 1838 by Wheatstone, who also devised the first stereoscope, which is an apparatus for presenting the appropriate picture to each eye. A simplified stereoscope is shown in (3).

In the stereograms shown in Figure 4–6 A to F, you can provide each eye with the appropriate picture by the following procedure: Place a small mirror on the gray center line. As indicated in (3), adjust the mirror until the picture seen in the mirror appears to lie in the same plane as does the picture seen directly. Then fixate the picture in the mirror, and wait for the stereo effect to develop. Proficiency will come quickly.

cal connections that are sensitive to the degree of disparity between the two images produced by a point in space; however, you should be cautioned that most theories about the exact nature of the binocular depth cues are still much more speculative, and based on more carefully selected evidence, than their authoritative tone would suggest.

The geometry of the retinal disparity of points in space has been subjected to a great deal of sophisticated analysis in an attempt to find the correspondence between perceived space and physical space. Such attempts start with the concept of *corresponding points,* points that would coincide if one retina could be slipped over the other (Figure 4-7): If a point in space projects its image to corresponding points on the retinas of the two eyes, a single point of light will be observed. As we shall see in Chapter 5, however, we can question whether such analyses in terms of *points* are appropriate to the perceptual process. In any event, we cannot accept binocularity as *the* basic depth cue upon which all space perception rests, since individuals who cannot use this cue at all well, may still show good spatial judgment. In fact, one-eyed individuals may display depth-perception at a very early age (see Figure 4-12B).

Moreover, binocular disparity, like the monocular cues, is also ambiguous, since we can receive any set of retinal images in at least two ways—by looking at the object, 1, or by looking at the stereogram, 2, in Figure 4-5B.

The Structuralist Theory of Space Perception

Having found visual cues that might provide information about the spatial locations of objects, we may then inquire concerning the physiological mechanisms by which we might use these cues. The earliest, easiest, and most persistent argument has been that there are no such mechanisms, that our observations of "space" are not visual at all, but consist of the kinesthetic memory images that have become

Figure 4-6. **Stereograms: three dimensions from two views.** *In (A) each eye receives a slightly different view of the two rings at (1). Although neither the left view (L) nor the right view (R), as shown at (2), contains any depth cue to indicate which ring is nearer, if you present each view to the appropriate eye using the stereogram at (3) (in which the right view has been reversed) and the procedure that is illustrated in Figure 4-5B3, the correct spatial arrangement will appear after a moment's viewing.*

The perception of a single three-dimensional scene is not simply a result of adding together the disparate views received by the two eyes. In (B1) no shape is recognizable in either view considered separately, nor can you detect any shape by looking for differences between the two views, but when the two patterns are viewed as a stereogram, a clearly visible object will appear, floating in space (Julesz). Such stereograms are prepared by starting with two identical patterns of dots (white) and then displacing an entire region (as shown at 2) in one of the

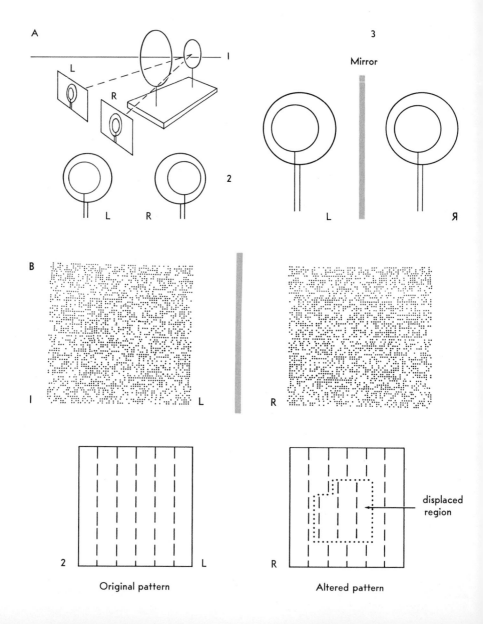

Original pattern   Altered pattern

patterns. Since the original pattern is random, the displacement of the region can not be detected simply by looking at the altered pattern; however, when the original is viewed by one eye and the altered pattern is viewed by the other, the displaced region then becomes visible, showing that the binocular visual system is directly sensitive to the differences in the stimulation at the two eyes. This sensitivity to binocular disparity is almost certainly innate. What happens when we set the cue of binocular disparity in conflict with one of the "secondary" or pictorial depth cues?

The two views at (C1) each contain the depth cue of interposition or overlap (see p. 35), which is in agreement with the cue of binocular disparity, as you will see if you view stereogram (2). When the two views are changed so that the left eye obtains the R view and vice versa, as in the pseudoscopic pair at (3), binocular disparity and interposition are in conflict. What disparity indicates as be-ing near, interposition shows to be far, and vice versa. Which cue wins out in (3)?

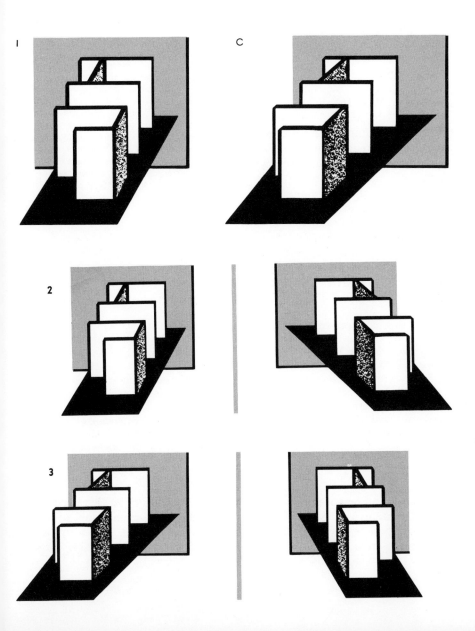

associated with the visual stimuli during our past experiences. This argument was advanced for two reasons: first, because all the static depth cues are ambiguous, as we saw on page 36; second, because the careful use of analytic introspection seemed to show that the only *visual* sensations that could be discovered were nonspatial and two-dimensional.

Let us consider this theory in somewhat more detail, because it dominated psychological thought for many years, and because it displays the structuralist approach most clearly.

Berkeley's New Theory of Vision.

How do the depth cues cause depth and distance to be observed? Whence do we get our ideas of space, size, solidity, and so on? Berkeley's now-traditional hypothesis was that only one such source *could* possibly exist, our memories of past experiences— hence the name *empiricist* (from empirical, meaning "founded on experience"), which is frequently used for this theory.

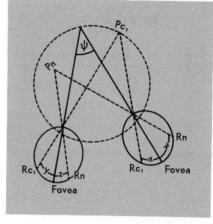

Figure 4-7. **Distance, disparity, and corresponding points.** *The points marked* (Rc_1) *are* corresponding *points, since each is the same distance from the fovea* $(x = y)$. *With the eyes converged as shown (angle* ψ*), the image of object* (Pc_1) *falls on corresponding retinal points* (Rc_1). *The retinal images of object* (Pn) *fall on points* (Rn) *that are noncorresponding, or* disparate $(z \neq w)$, *and this disparity offers a cue to the distance between* (Pc_1) *and* (Pn).

Here is the heart of this theory, Berkeley's extremely influential argument in his own words:

> . . . the judgment we make of the distance of an object . . . is entirely the result of experience . . . a man born blind, being made to see, would at first have no idea of Distance by sight: the sun and stars, the remotest objects as well as the nearer, would all seem to be in his eye, or rather in his mind . . . each . . . as near to him as the perceptions of pain or pleasure, or the most inward passions of his soul. . . . And I believe whoever will look narrowly into his own thoughts, and examine what he means by saying that he sees this or that thing at a distance, will agree with me, that what he sees only *suggests* to his understanding that, after having passed a certain distance, *to be measured by the motion of the body, which is perceivable by touch,* he shall come to perceive such and such tangible ideas [i.e., sensations of touch].

The Nonvisual Components of Visual Space.

According to this hypothesis, then, an infant first learns the idea of distance by a combination of visual and kinesthetic experiences. The toy he wishes to grasp is, say, a full arm's reach away from him, and subtends at that distance a visual angle of, say,

10° (Figure 4-8A); by accident, perhaps, he extends his arm the full distance and grasps the toy to him. At another time, with the toy a half-arm's reach away, it subtends a visual angle of, say 30° (Figure 4-8B). After many such experiences, it is reasoned, the child needs only to glance at the toy in order to recall either the half-bent arm or the fully-extended arm when the corresponding size of image falls upon his retina. From this viewpoint, the observation of distance *always* rests on the memory images of previous kinesthetic experiences.

But reaching or walking to an object are not the only kinesthetic contributions to depth perception. Our eyes also move, and their muscular system can contribute to the observation of visual distance most directly in the mechanisms of accomodation and convergence. For any point in space at any moderate distance from the eye, the lens must be stretched or relaxed to some degree which is precisely related to that distance, in order to bring the point to a sharp focus on the retina. This process is called *accommodation*. Similarly, the eyes must *converge* at some angle, which is precisely related to the distance of the point, in order to bring the retinal image of that point to the fovea of each eye (these mechanisms were shown in Figures 3-3 and 3-15). These adjustments undoubtedly do occur. If we could sense the degree of tension in the muscles responsible for these adjustments, we would have an additional set of depth cues. For these two nonvisual cues are closely tied to

Figure 4-8. **The muscle-movement theory of visual space.** *The most influential theory of space perception in Western thought has been that distance is not a direct visual sensation at all. Instead, the empiricist theory maintains, when the retinal image of some object brings to mind the memories of the grasping or walking motions that have been made in the past in order to reach that object, those memories provide the idea of "distance."*

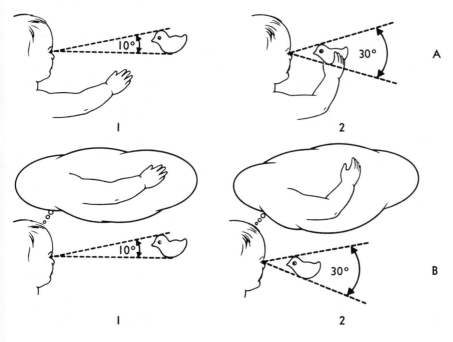

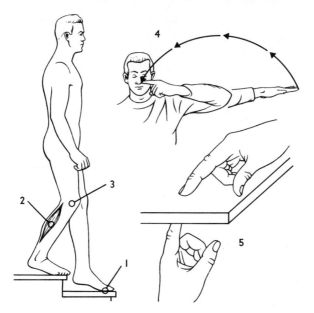

Figure 4-9. Locating the body in visual space: the kinesthetic and proprioceptive senses. Three types of receptors that are sensitive to pressure and strain are distributed as follows: over the body surfaces as the tactile sense organs of the skin (1); within the muscle bundles (2), to provide the kinesthetic system with information about the contractions of the muscles; and in the joints (3), to provide the proprioceptive information about the relative positions and displacements of the skeletal framework. Taken together with the senses of balance and acceleration (see Figure 4-10) they contribute to the body image (4, 5): The body image provides a spatial framework within which muscular behaviors are coordinated. Victims of diseases (such as locomotor ataxia) that have destroyed parts of the body image must guide each individual bodily movement visually, as in looking at each foot to see that it makes the proper movements for walking. To get an idea of the precision of this body image as a spatial framework, try the following tasks: (4) Close your eyes, stretch one arm to the side, at shoulder height, then bring index finger of that arm in to touch the tip of your nose in one smooth motion. (5) Place the index finger of your left hand against the underside of a tabletop, out of sight, then place the index finger of your right hand on the topside of the table immediately over it.

spatial distance. It is easy to imagine circumstances, in which any of the pictorial depth cues would be wrong, but "fooling" accommodation or convergence requires special apparatus. Sensations resulting from these actions *can* be observed, with only a little effort. For instance, change your fixation rapidly from the horizon to the tip of your nose, and you will feel both sets of muscles in action. For these reasons, accommodation and convergence were thought to be primary depth cues in visual space perception, even though they are not visual at all. If so, our observations of spatial distance would then consist of three elements: kinesthetic sensations from the muscles of accomodation and convergence; plus those memories of the previous kinesthetic sensations of reaching or walking that had become associated with the specific accommodation and convergence sensations; and, finally, the "pure" visual sensations such as the color patches we discussed in Chapter 3.

Locating the Observer in Space and with Respect to Gravity. So far, we have explained how we might observe the distance that some point is from our eyes, but normally we don't see things as being more or less distant from *us*—instead, we see things as being at some place *in space,* and we also perceive our bodies to be at some specific place within the same spatial framework. Can we account for this spatial framework in structuralist terms?

We have already discussed the localization of a point in space with respect to our eyes; we also need to be able to sense the localization of our eyes with respect to the rest of our bodies, and to observe the position of our bodies with respect to gravity. The sensory systems diagrammed in Figures 4-9 and 4-10, respectively, would appear to be capable of providing this sensory information, and we know that our perceptions of the main directions of space do draw upon these systems. In addition to sight and kinesthesis, our ears offer us information about the spatial location of objects (Figure 4-11). The immense amount of concomitant experience we get through these separate sensory systems is constantly being coordinated by the consistent physical world which surounds us and which is the underlying source of stimulation, uniting these unrelated masses of sensations in one structure of associations.

This is the structuralist explanation of our perceptions of the spatial world, and it appeared to provide an elegant and unified foundation upon which to build an understanding of other more complex psychological processes.

Convincing though this argument has been for centuries, it faces some grave difficulties. Perhaps most striking is the fact that at least some creatures can make good spatial discriminations without ever having previously associated kinesthetic images to the visual cues (Figure 4-12), and most of the kinds of creatures (including human infants) that have been tested in a recent series of experiments with the *visual cliff*, appear to be capable of some depth-discrimination as soon as they are old enough to move around at all. These facts don't prove that *all* space perception is innate (see Figure 4-13). They do make Berkeley's logical argument, that space perception *must* be learned, quite unconvincing.

THE PERCEPTION OF THE QUALITIES AND MOTIONS OF OBJECTS

So far, we have dealt mostly with points in space. Let us now try to assemble them into the objects of the world around us.

Imagine a flat mosaic, like a tile floor, built of sensitive elements—this is a structuralist model of the retina. Let the light reflected from an object produce an image on the retina, covering some of these sensitive receptor elements. Each element is sensitive to light, and the more intensely each is stimulated, the *brighter* the observed object should be. With a greater visual angle subtended at the eye, a larger area will be stimulated, and the observed *size* should increase. What about *shape* and *motion*?

Any shape that falls on the retina is, by this theory, simply a particular arrangement of points or patches; some of these arrangements have occurred so frequently together that all the parts are associated to each other and to the verbal names we have given to them (such as, "circle" or "face").*

* Until relatively recently, it was believed that the observation of shape was made possible only by the kinesthetic sensations caused by eye movements made while the fovea follows the outline of the shape. Despite a number of demonstrations that *tachistoscopic exposures* of shapes (that is, presentations too short to permit eye movement to occur) still allow the shapes to be discriminated, this belief still reappears from time to time. Many people seem to find explanations of vision in terms of muscular movements particularly satisfying.

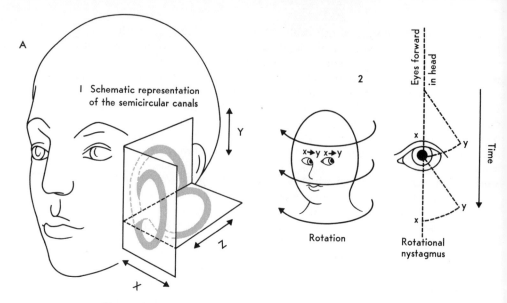

Figure 4-10. **Orientation and acceleration.** (A) The organs of equilibrium are located in the inner ear near the cochlea, which is the organ of hearing. The semicircular canals (1) provide information to the nervous system each time a movement of the head along one or more of the three dimensions of space agitates the fluid in the appropriate canals. Other organs, called the vestibular sacs, respond with each tilt of the head against the downward pull of gravity. These organs are nicely suited to respond to changes in orientation or in velocity, and to provide the other sensory systems with the raw material needed to maintain a constant frame of reference with respect to the earth, even though the head on which those other organs are mounted is in continual movement. For example, if you whirl around like an ice skater or a ballet dancer, impulses from these organs set the eyes into an automatic compensatory reflex movement (called a nystagmus), which acts to help keep the retinal image still as long as possible during each glance at the world (2). If (x) is the straight-ahead direction in the head, the eye travels toward (y) against the motion of rotation, then rapidly snaps back in the direction of rotation and repeats the movement. Because of the nausea which attends any disturbance of these organs, and because of their importance in setting the spatial framework of perception, we could not be certain that normal perception would be possible in the absence of gravity ("free fall"). But recent prolonged orbital flights by U.S. and U.S.S.R. astronauts have shown that coordinated perception continues to be possible.

(B) The fact is that our perceptions of the main direction of space do not depend completely on our organs of equilibrium and proprioception. Our visual environments usually contain obvious axes of vertical and horizontal orientation, such as walls, trees, and floors, and these provide a purely visual spatial co-ordinate system. The task of the observer in (B) is to adjust his chair until it is vertical, and his final setting is usually a compromise between the axis of gravity (G) and the main visual axis (V) (Witkin et al.).

Although there are great individual differences in the accuracy of performance on this task, the visual directions can readily be made to override the effects of gravitation (C). The "magic swing" occasionally found in amusement parks is a stationary suspended chair. The room (1) swings back and forth from (X) to (Y), around the observer. Such an enclosing visual framework exerts an extremely strong tendency to be seen at rest (see Figure 5-14), and, in consequence, the observer feels himself swinging to and fro, between (Y) and (X), as shown in (2)—to the extent that, if the room revolves completely, he will feel himself turning head over heels while the room appears to remain fixed and stationary!

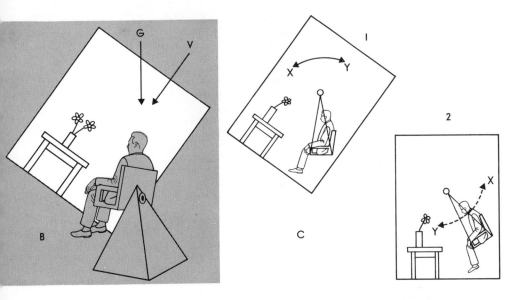

Figure 4-11. **The auditory bases of space: stereophonic localization and other distance cues.** *In vision, the perception of spatial direction seems easy enough to explain: Because the retina is spread out in space, light from different spatial directions will fall upon different receptors. In hearing, the perception of spatial direction involves other mechanisms. Analogous to binocular disparity, the two ears receive pressure-waves differently from different places in space. (A) The pressure-waves reach the nearer ear first, and this disparity, d (together with other binaural differences, such as the fact that a slightly lower intensity of stimulation reaches the farther ear because of a "sound shadow" cast by the head) permits the observer to localize the direction from which the sound is coming. (B) Just as*

a stereoscope can present different pictures to each eye and thereby produce a three-dimensional effect, a stereophonic sound-reproduction system can present appropriate binaural disparities and recreate many of the apparent spatial separations of the original recording session. The pressure waves of the violin reach the right ear first, those of the drum reach the left ear first, and the horn reaches both ears together—as it should, since it is straight ahead during the recording session. This spatial separation permits a better appreciation of the contribution of each instrument than can usually be obtained in a monaural recording. The differences in arrival time are very slight—about 1/1000 of a second. The time that it takes for the sounds of one's breathing and of one's footsteps to be reflected from the surfaces around one (about 1/1000 of a second for each additional 6 inches of distance from the reflecting surface) provides the basis for what used to be called "facial vision" in blind subjects, enabling them to locate surfaces in space by ear. Some animals (especially the bat) depend almost entirely on this means of avoiding obstacles in space: Such creatures emit high-frequency sound-waves and are guided by the time it takes the echoes to return.

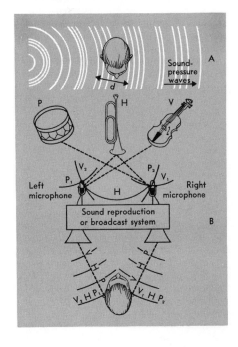

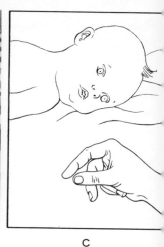

A   B   C

Figure 4-12. **Space discriminations without prior visuomotor experience.** *(A) Chicks that were hatched and reared in darkness and therefore have had no opportunity to form visual-kinesthetic associations can, nevertheless, use visual depth cues when first exposed to them: When they are placed on test stands in an illuminated space, the higher the stand, the longer they delay in jumping (Thorndike). (B) A variety of animals—including human infants—display a similar ability as soon as they are old enough to locomote at all. When placed on the center of a glass sheet, with patterned linoleum up against the glass on one side of the mid-line and a drop-off in a sheer "visual cliff" on the other, they avoid the cliff, indicating the use of purely visual depth cues (Gibson and Walk). A child who had been essentially one-eyed from birth, displayed the same choice on the visual cliff at age 18 months, a finding which makes the claim that binocular disparity is fundamental to space perception (p. 39) very dubious (Walk and Dodge). (C) We cannot rear human infants in darkness. However, in an extremely ingenious experiment with an infant delivered without drugs, it was found that the baby would turn consistently toward the source of a sound, only moments after birth, a fact that establishes the existence of some minimum amount of spatially coordinated behavior at the time of delivery (Wertheimer).*

Standard
for 4-14

Figure 4-13. **The kitten carousel.** *We should not conclude from the experiments of Figure 4-12 that the visuomotor experience is not involved at all in the development of space perception. Kittens were paired in the carousel so that one was passive and the other active. The latter wheeled the passive partner around in the light for one hour, while the remainder of the day was spent in darkness. Both animals thus received the same amount of visual stimulation. The passive cats showed marked inabilities on the visual cliff and in other visual tasks which require depth perception and visuomotor coordination. The active partners showed no such deficit (Held and Hein).*

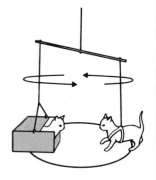

Perceiving
Objects
as Structures
of Sensations

Motion would be observed whenever a succession of neighboring receptors were stimulated. Neither shape nor motion, then, seems to require the structuralist to seek any additional explanations. All the physical properties of the world of objects that we see, are thus accounted for—but with some surprising peculiarities:

If we introspect carefully, the visual sensations of every object's properties should appear to vary from one moment to the next, in an astonishing manner. Size, shape, brightness—all change drastically in the optic array and in the retinal image, as the observer and the objects he looks at move about in the world (Figure 4-14), and so, therefore, should our observations change.

Do we really observe the world in this inconsistent fashion? In fact, we see the physical attributes of objects both *more* correctly, and *less* correctly, than we should expect from what we know about sensory psychophysics. The basic structuralist attempt to observe the component sensations has failed for

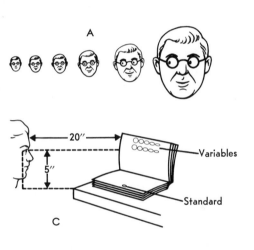
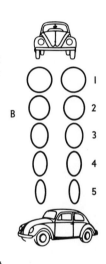

Figure 4-14. Size constancy and shape constancy. *(A) The approximate change in size in the retinal image of a friend's face, as he approaches on the street. If you hold your thumb up at about eye level and move it to and fro, from close to your eye out to arm's length and back again, it will continue to appear roughly constant in size, that is, "thumb size" —unless you pay attention to the objects that it hides from view at different distances. At arm's length, the tip of your thumb can hide your friend's nose at four feet; it can hide his head at 20 feet; it can hide him completely at 150 feet. Does your friend appear to shrink to thumb-tip size when he is 150 feet away? Again, when your thumb approaches from arm's length to about three inches, the image of its tip in the optic array expands from being able to cover your friend's head, to hiding his entire body. Does your thumb appear to swell from head size to body size? (B) Headlights of a passing automobile provide retinal images that vary from the perfect circle of a head-on view, through an ellipse of ever-narrowing proportions, to a sliver of light. Do you normally detect these changes in shape? (C) Try the following experiment, however: Turn the book around so that you are facing it from the distances and at the orientation shown and then attempt to match the appearance of the standard circle, shown on the facing page, to the series of ellipses in (B). Which one of the ellipses matches the standard in retinal image? See the note on the bottom of page 51 for the answer.*

every physical attribute of objects that has been studied. We can list these failures under three headings: the *perceptual constancies*, the *illusions*, and the facts of *organization*.

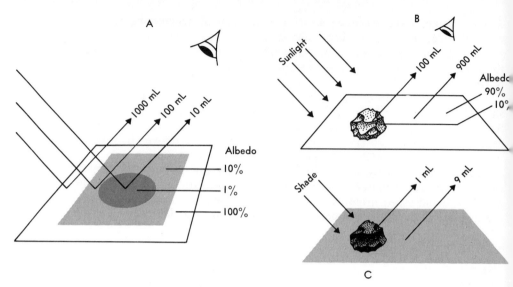

Figure 4-15. **Lightness constancy.** *(A) Even though the intensity of the light-energy reaching the eye may change greatly from one moment to the next as the illumination on an object changes from direct sunlight to deep shadow, the apparent lightness of the object will remain relatively constant and unchanged. The light-energy reflected or omitted by some surface is measured in units called millilamberts. (B) In sunlight, coal may reflect 100 millilamberts (mL) of light-energy, and paper, 900 mL. (C) In the shade, the coal may reflect 1 mL, the paper, 9 mL. Does the paper look darker in the shade than the coal did in the sunlight? No: The coal looks black, and the paper looks white, regardless of the light each reflects to the eye.*

The Perceptual Constancies

The world we see is, by and large, a stable one. Only in unusual circumstances can we detect the tremendous changes of size in proximal stimulation as we walk about, and the changes in the light reaching our eye from any object as the illumination changes.* Most generally a friend does *not* appear to double in size with each couple of steps; the headlights on a car do not seem to turn from circles through elipses to lines as they pass us on the road (Figure 4-14); and the lump of coal does not change from black to white when it moves from shade to sunlight (Figure 4-15). Object characteristics appear to remain approximately constant, even though the corresponding proximal stimulation changes. These general phenomena are variously called the object constancies, phenomenal constancies, or perceptual constancies.

It is tempting, therefore, to explain the constancies as mechanisms by which the observer "achieves" veridical, correct observations of the world,

* There is something that does in fact remain constant in the retinal image in each instance of the constancies; we shall consider what does remain constant later on (pp. 75, 80).

because they are so necessary to his effective actions and survival. This only recognizes the utility of the constancies, however; it does not explain how they come to be. Let us examine two important examples of the constancies and the structuralist attempt to explain these pervasive phenomena.

Lightness Constancy * and Memory Color.   When light-energy falls upon the surface of an object, some of the energy is reflected and some is absorbed (or transmitted, if the object is transparent). Under normal circumstances, if the object reflects most of the light, it is usually seen as white; an object that fails to reflect any light at all appears black. The percentage of the light a surface reflects is its *albedo,* and we observe this physical characteristic with surprising accuracy, *even though the amount of light actually reaching the eye, from that object, may vary widely* (Figure 4-15).

The most obvious explanation is that we *know* the colors of coal and of paper, and that this knowledge (the *memory colors* of coal and paper) influences our judgments. This answer, though obvious, is wrong, since lightness constancy is obtained perfectly well with objects of unknown albedo. Somehow we must be taking into account the following complicated facts.

Consider an object that projects a certain specific amount of light to the eye. In order to project that amount of light, it must be a darker object if it is in full illumination than if it is in partial (or lower) illumination (Figure 4-15). Consequently, if the object appears to be in the shade, it will also appear to be lighter than if—without any change in the light reaching the eye—it appears to be brightly lit. If this complicated kind of calculation were really being made each time we observe the lightness of a surface, would we not notice that we are making it? This same question arises in every one of the constancies.

Size Constancy and Familiar Size.   The tremendous changes in size an object's image undergoes in the optic array, as the object itself moves around in space, are illustrated in Figure 4-14. These size changes are not usually noticeable in normal visual perception. The observed size tends to remain constant, in spite of them. See Figure 4-16.† This tendency for the apparent

---

* Lightness and brightness are not identical. Lightness is the continuum running from white surface to black surface. Brightness is the apparent amount of light coming from the object; thus a piece of coal in the sunlight and a piece of coal in the shade will be of equal lightness, if constancy is perfect, but the coal in the sunlight will appear much brighter.

† Figure 4-16 is a picture, which complicates the problem. In a picture (which is almost equivalent to the proximal stimulation which would be received from a real scene), V3 = S *both* as a proximal *and* as a distal match, since S and V are really at the same distance from the eye. Constancy experiments can be performed with pictures by using the represented distance instead of the real distance when computing constancy ratios, with quite reliable results. If you look at the scene in Figure 4-16A through a tunnel of a rolled-up paper for a few moments, you will most probably find that V2 or V1 seems much closer in size to S, than does V3. (See G. Sonoda. Perceptual constancies observed in plane pictures. *Bulletin of the faculty of literature of Kyushu University,* No. 7, 1961, pp. 199–228).

NOTE: The answer to the question in Figure 4-14C: Ellipse 5 is closest in shape.

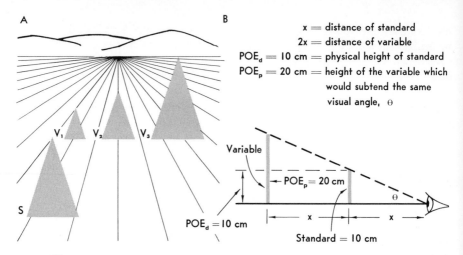

Figure 4-16. Constancy ratios. (A) Look at the scene through a tube of rolled-up paper, or through a hole punched in a sheet of cardboard so that your field of view is restricted to the picture itself. Which of the variables (V_1, V_2, and V_3) appears to be equal in size to the standard (S)? In the real situation, represented by this picture, most observers will pick a value close to (V_2). Note that in the real situation, there would be two POE's, or points of objective equality, in which (S) and (V) are objectively equal, as measured physically. One POE is obtained when (S) and (V) subtend equal visual angles of the eye. This is the POE_p, which is called a proximal match, because the it refers to a choice of (V) at which the two proximal stimuli are the same size. A second POE is obtained when (S) and (V) are equal in size as physical objects. This is the POE_d, or distal match, because it refers to a choice of (V) whereby (S) and (V) are equal as distal stimuli. One measure of perceptual constancy is the constancy ratio, $C = (PSE - POE_p)/ (POE_d - POE_p)$. In this measure, the PSE is the point of subjective equality, that is, the value of (V) at which the observer decides that the standard and variable are equal (using one of the psychophysical methods, p. 8). POE_p is the setting at which the standard and variable produce the same retinal image or proximal stimulus (here, V_3); and POE_d is the setting at which the standard and variable are equal as distal objects (here, V_2). (B) In the size-constancy experiment represented here, if PSE = 10, $C = (10-20)/(10-20) = 1.0$, which would mean that the match is being made solely in terms of the distal sizes of (S) and (V), and size constancy would be perfect. Most usually, some intermediate value is obtained.

size of an object to remain constant while the proximal stimulus changes in size is called size constancy; the term also includes the related tendency to see large objects as large and small objects as small even when their proximal stimulus sizes are the same (Figure 4-17A). Why do we see the man as being taller than the boy in Figure 4-17B?

Analogous to the explanation offered for color constancy in terms of memory color, we might suppose that size constancy occurs because we *know* the true, physical sizes of men and boys. This is the traditional cue of *familiar size* (see p. 35). Yet size constancy is also obtained for entirely unfamiliar objects. Moreover, by the use of false perspective (Figure 4-17C), we can fool the eye into accepting two perfectly familiar, equal-sized objects as being the same distances when they are really at different distances. The objects that would normally appear constant in size then appear greatly different, as one would expect from the distance framework in which they are set, *not* as one would expect from their familiar size. As a cue, familiar size (or the size you know an object to be) is not good, and we shall see that there is some question about whether it can work at all.

Alternatively, we might try to explain size constancy on the basis that an object's distance is somehow taken into account, just as we might try to explain lightness constancy as the result of taking illumination into account. That is, perhaps the *size of an object is computed from the size of its retinal image, and from its apparent distance,* just as an astronomer can compute the positions of the stars in space using trigonometry or a surveyor can calculate the distance to some landmark.

This is also an appealing possibility and is still widely accepted, but we must qualify it immediately: The observer is *not aware* of making such computations if he does make them at all. The implications of this fact must be

Figure 4-17. The effects of context on apparent size. (A) Are the cylinders at (1) and (2) the same size? (B) Are the boy and man the same size? If you measure the heights with a ruler, you will find them the same in both cases. (C) Now consider the two men here. Both men are of normal height, but one of them is considerably nearer. The room, of course, is quite distorted; looked at from above, it is shaped as shown in (D). To monocular vision, however, the room appears to be rectangular, and our familiarity with the sizes of the two men are not sufficient to overcome this "assumption of rectangularity." If the room were in reality rectangular, the view would be that shown in (E). How is (C) related to (A) and (B)? (See Ittelson and Kilpatrick.)

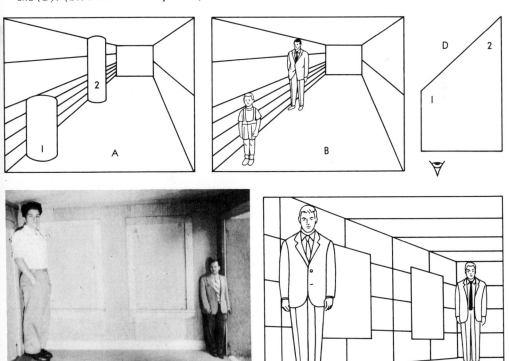

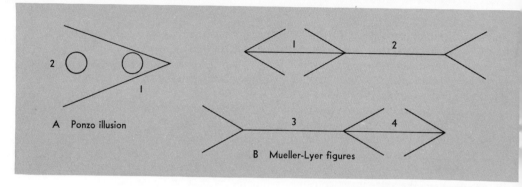

A Ponzo illusion

B Mueller-Lyer figures

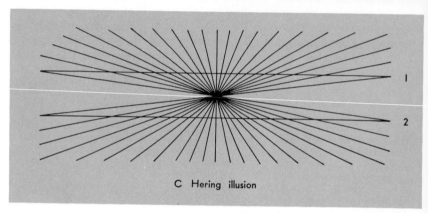

C Hering illusion

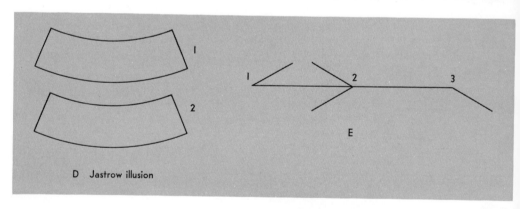

D Jastrow illusion

E

Figure 4-18. The geometrical illusions: erroneous perceptions of size and place. (A) Circles (1) and (2) are really the same size. (B) Segments (1), (2), (3), and (4) are all the same size. (C) The two horizontal lines are parallel, the distance between (1) and (2) being the same all the way across the figure. (D) The two crescents (1) and (2) are the same size. (E) This figure is explained in the text.

There are a great many different illusions of this general class, in which what you perceive corresponds neither to the proximal stimulus nor to the distal object. In general, they are even stronger than the constancies, to which at least some of them may be related. What is the common factor in Figures 4-18A, 4-17E and 4-16A?

Perceiving
Objects
as Structures
of Sensations

considered in some detail, since they strike at the heart of the entire structuralist approach.

Unconscious Conclusions from Unnoticed Sensations To Explain Perceptual Achievement.　　This hypothesis of unconscious computation, or *unconscious inference,* implies that *sensations cannot in fact be observed but that instead they are hidden, or overlaid, by the unconsciously achieved conclusions.* This explanation faces a number of difficulties but it remains the most serious empiricist attempt to explain the fact that our observations are usually more like the distal objects of the real world than like the sensations we would expect from the proximal stimulation (and from our knowledge of sensory psychophysics). It can explain perceptual achievement only if we abandon the belief that we can continue to observe the individual sensations.

　　Can it explain the other two kinds of discrepancies between proximal stimulation and appearance, namely illusions and organizations?

Illusions

For every example of constancy and perceptual achievement we can find an illusion or perceptual error, that has a greater discrepancy with the distal world than we would expect from the proximal stimulation. Figure 4-16 was an example of size constancy, yet Figure 4-18A is considered an illusion; Figure 4-15 is an example of lightness-constancy, yet Figure 4-19 is an illusion.

　　Several kinds of illusions are illustrated in Figure 4-18; others appear in later pages. These are not simple cases of careless observation that can be countered by taking pains. The only way in which most illusions can be detected as such in these figures is by taking a ruler and measuring them. If no means of predicting their effects or of anticipating their occurrence can be found, the scientific study of perception will be impossible. Consequently, we cannot dismiss illusions as mere curiosities which demonstrate that "one can't trust one's senses."

Two Famous Illusions of Size Inconstancy: The Mueller-Lyer Illusion and the Moon Illusion.　　Many explanations have been offered to account for the illu-

Figure 4-19. Color contrast: erroneous perceptions of brightness and hue. In (A) the two halves of the gray ring are really identical, as we see when we view the ring without the split background in (B). Contrast will also induce illusory changes in hue: In (A) if (1) and (2) were red and green respectively, (3) and (4) would appear greenish and reddish, respectively. See also the "colored shadows" of Figure 5-2A. In general, color contrast results in induction of the complementary hue (the opposites on the color circle in Figure 3-9A).

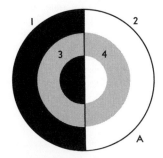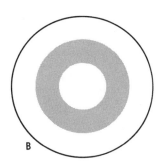

sions.* According to the perspective theory of the Mueller-Lyer illusion, for example, the "converging lines" at 1 and 2 in Figure 4-18E, have been thought to "suggest" the depth cue of linear perspective. Therefore, it has been reasoned, segment 1-2 appears nearer than segment 2-3; since 1-2 appears near while subtending the same visual angle, it should appear *shorter* than 2-3. This would explain the illusion as being due to the *unconscious* use of a depth cue where there is, in fact, no real depth.

At first glance this doesn't make sense. Shouldn't an object appear to be larger if it appears to be nearer than it really is? Not according to the following reasoning (known in recent years as the *size-distance invariance* hypothesis).

Examine Figure 4-20B. In order to maintain a given visual angle θ (and, therefore, a given retinal image size) as the distance of the distal stimulus increases, so must its physical size increase. In fact, where S = stimulus size, d = stimulus distance, and k = tan θ, $S = k \times d$.

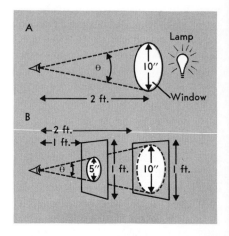

This is a simple physical invariance, that is easily demonstated by the procedure shown in Figure 4-20. If, as a result of learning (or by native endowment), our perceptions of the world agree with its physical characteristics, we should expect to to find a *perceptual invariance* intimately related to this physical invariance. *For a given proximal stimulus (θ), as apparent distance increases, apparent size should increase and vice versa.*†

Now we can return to the "perspective explanation" of the Mueller-Lyer illusion shown in Figure

Figure 4-20. Size-distance invariance hypothesis and Emmert's Law. Prolonged staring at a light produces an afterimage (p. 23). If an afterimage is obtained by gazing at the bright window in (A), and then projected on the one-foot-square paper in (B), it will cover an area 10 inches across at a distance of two feet. If you now move the paper to a distance of one foot, how large is the afterimage? The size of a projected afterimage is directly proportional to the distance from the eye to the surface upon which the image is projected. This is known as Emmert's Law.

* One recurrent explanation is that these illusions are due to the effects of eye movements. For example, our eyes make an unbroken sweep across length 1-2, Figure 4-18B, but are prevented from doing the same for 1. Unfortunately for this explanation, tachistoscopic exposures in too short a time to permit eye movements, result in a strong illusion anyway.

† This *invariance of two distal measures for a fixed proximal measure* holds not only for *size and distance* but for such other physical properties as *lightness and illumination, slant-and-shape,* that is, for all the attributes which display the constancies. This may be a clue to what remains constant in the constancies, and we shall return to some of these other invariances later (p. 74).

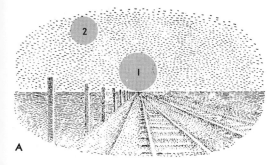
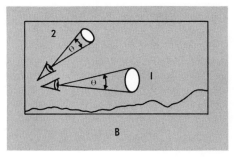

Figure 4-21. The "moon illusion." (A) The moon seems much larger when it is near the horizon (1) than when it is overhead (2). Although several factors (such as the elevation of your gaze; see Holway and Boring) contribute to this effect, recent research supports an ancient explanation: Distance cues in the terrain immediately adjacent to the horizon moon help cause the illusion, making the horizon look larger by making it look farther away (Kaufman and Rock). (B) This illusion can easily be demonstrated in daylight. Obtain an after-image by looking at a bright light, and then project it on the sky. Near the horizon (1), it appears larger than when it is projected overhead (2), even though the proximal stimulus (visual angle θ) remains constant (Gruber and King). Look back at Emmert's law (Figure 4-20). What do these facts seem to imply about the distance of the sky at horizon and at zenith?

4-18E. Since the retinal size of the horizontal segment 2 remains constant, a *decrease* in apparent distance should result in a *decrease* in apparent size.

This explanation would also apply to many other size illusions; consider the famous moon illusion (shown in Figure 4-21).

It has been known for thousands of years that the moon looks larger when it is near the horizon (1 in the Figure) than when it is overhead at its zenith (2), even though the visual angle subtended by the moon remains constant. Why does this illusion occur? One of the earliest explanations, which now has some experimental support, was that the sky at the horizon looks farther away (due to the intervening terrain), and thus the moon seems larger near the horizon. Once again, the observer seems somehow to take the distance into account in judging the object's size, by some sort of unconscious inference.

Unconscious Inferences. The principle of unconscious inference does seem to explain the illusions as well as the constancies—at least as a first approximation. If such inferences do explain these illusions, however, they are *not* calculations that the observer can report, nor do they depend on *knowledge* in any simple sense of the word. Knowing that the Mueller-Lyer illusion lies on a flat surface does not dispel the illusion; knowing that the moon remains the same size does not affect the moon illusion. Moreover, the quantitative measurements of the illusions—the precise extents of the errors as measured in psychophysical experiments—do not agree exactly with what we would expect to find in accordance with this principle.

For these reasons, unconscious inference is really only an approximate rule of thumb. We shall consider alternate explanations later on.

Perceiving
Objects
as Structures
of Sensations

The Perception of Shape and Motion:
A First Introduction
to the Principles of Organization

As we have just seen, the illusions and the constancies reveal discrepancies between what we should observe if sensations are simply added together, on the one hand, and what we do in fact observe, on the other. Discrepancies become overwhelming when we turn to the perception of shape and of motion. The sensations seem to become completely unobservable, and totally submerged in the over-all organization of the perceived object—if they are present at all in *any* sense.

Camouflage and Puzzle-Pictures. In the structuralist scheme, a shape is simply the sum of the sensations of points of color and shade at a particular set of positions (see Figure 4-1C). In Figure 4-22A are a number of familiar shapes in plain view. Can you see them? Is this concealment due to the confusion caused by the added lines? No, this cannot be the answer, since in Figure 4-22B the same patterns of stimulation are now embedded among even more lines (or suffer even more omissions) yet are clearly observable.

Figure 4-22. Camouflage and puzzle-pictures: invisibility through "organization." Various numbers and letters are concealed in (1), (2), and (3) in (A) (after Köhler). Why are they invisible there, yet obvious in (1), (2), and (3) in (B)? In (C) there are two pencils (after Metzger). Which is easier to see, the one that is partly covered, or the one that is completely uncovered? An entire animal is concealed in (D).

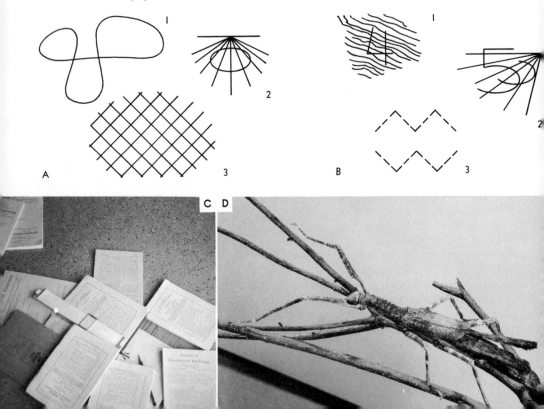

A

Figure 4-23. Figure and ground, visibility and invisibility. (A) A set of Fiji island charms? A word is "concealed" here. In general, what is "figure" has a recognizable shape, while what is "ground" does not. (B) You can either see as figure a black goblet standing in front of a white ground, or you can see two white faces, looking at each other, in front of a black ground. If you think that you see both, you are probably either alternating between the two or you see one region of the contour as part of a white profile, and another region as part of a black vase. See Chapter 5 for other examples.

B

Is this somehow due to the artificiality of lines on paper, or to human habits of looking at them? No, for we find the same principles of concealment used by animals to hide from other animals in the real world (Figure 4-22D; see also Figure 1-2C), and by pencils to hide from students (Figure 4-22C). What makes these sets of local sensations unobservable, in these combinations, even though their components are clearly above threshold when considered one at a time?

Is this simply a matter of seeing the shapes we have learned to see? No, again. The demonstrations in Figures 4-22 and 4-23A show that *what we might call familiar shape is no better a predictor of what we will see, than were memory color and familiar size.* The explanation for observed shape is *not* simply that certain specific shapes have been learned. There are evidently *laws of organization* at work—factors that depend on the relationships between the parts of the patterns of stimulation.

These laws of organization form the heart of *Gestalt* theory, which is an alternative to structuralism that we shall examine later, and they shall be considered in a more positive and detailed fashion in the next chapter. What makes them important to us here is this: Their demonstrations show quite dramatically that how we will perceive a whole object cannot be predicted simply

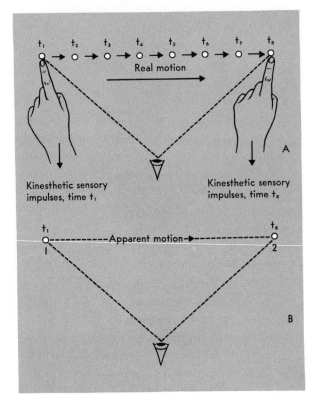

Figure 4-24. The perception of continuous motion. (A) The simplest way to explain the perception of motion would seem at first to be that we experience a sequence of successive visual sensations, each at a different position, plus the memories of previous tactual-kinesthetic sensations received when reaching out to the different positions. (B) In fact, however, if lights are turned on and off at (1) and (2) at suitable intervals, perceived motion occurs from (1) to (2). This phi phenomenon, which results from such interrupted presentation, may actually be more convincing than "real" or continuous movement of the stimulus, and provides the basis for TV and motion pictures. In the products of these major industries, no movement is present in either the distal or proximal stimulation, yet clear and continuous perceptions of motion result.

by adding up our perceptions of the parts, and that, indeed, the parts may become unobservable when combined with other parts.

The Perception of Motion.   The simplest structuralist explanation of our observations of motion was that perceived motion is simply composed of the *sensations of successive positions*, accompanied by the memory images of having touched the object by the use of different sets of body motions (Figure 4-24A). Are such sequential sensations necessary for the perception of motion? Not at all. We can observe perfectly convincing motion when no such successive stimulation occurs on the retina, as is shown by the *phi phenomenon* of Figure 4-24B. Again, this phenomenon of apparent motion is not simply a laboratory curiosity which depends on careful conditions of presentation or attitude. All motion pictures, TV, and animated displays are examples of this principle. A series of still photographs or drawings is presented in brief, *stationary* exposures or "frames," and the observation of motion is overwhelming. No one can see the individual frames in a movie regardless of how carefully he introspects.

Analytic introspection clearly will not work as intended. This failure has enormous consequences—not only for the study of perception but for the entire complex scientific enterprise of understanding man's sensory system. In a nutshell, the whole interlocking structure of sensory physiology, sensory psychophysics, and analytic perception has had some of its main assumptions pulled out from under it. We can no longer pursue old programs based upon these assumptions, and we have to understand the precise extent of the failures if we are to understand new programs in the study of perception. For new they must be, though they also must conserve what we have learned up to this point.

The Failures of Introspective Structuralism

The structuralist procedure for studying perception was to discover the underlying fundamental sensations and their physiological bases (or specific nerve energies), and the laws by which these elements combine. All other qualities for which we can find no receptors (such as distance, solidity, social attributes, facial expressions, and so forth) were to be built up out of these units. These elements were to combine with each other by simple addition. Other qualities presumably arise through bringing to mind the images left by earlier sensations, in accordance with the laws of association. This over-all viewpoint gave a general purpose to the enterprise of sensory psychophysics and provided a unified picture of man and of his perceptions of the world.

The basic failures lay in the addition hypothesis, in the technique of analytic introspection, or in both. We have examined all the building blocks (color, position, shape, size, and so on) for visual perception, and in each case, we find that the data of sensory psychophysics do not predict the observations made when those supposed building blocks are combined (pp. 50–60).

In many cases, we might explain the discrepancies from the addition hypothesis as being due to unconscious inferences that we make, based on our past experiences; we saw several examples of this in pp. 53–57. These explanations, whatever else they might do, cannot save analytic introspection, however, since with no amount of introspective effort can you overcome the effects of context and of past experiences, and detect the "true" sensation (for example, that the lines are really equal in the Mueller-Lyer illusion on p. 3).

However, if analytic introspection will not serve to dissect our perceptions of the world into the innate sensations, on the one hand, and memory images, on the other, how can we discover what is learned and what is innate? How can we investigate the empiricist assertion (see pp. 42–44) that the complex objects that we perceive are built up out of simpler sensory elements by some process of perceptual learning?

Perceiving
Objects
as Structures
of Sensations

Some form of empiricism is still tenable. We may continue to suppose that there are simple sensory elements (like those studied in sensory psychophysics), which are combined by the effects of our past experiences into the complex things we see. However, since we must now recognize that introspection simply cannot serve to observe either these elements, or their memory images from the past, the only way to know what associations any observer has formed is to discover what he has been exposed to in the past. One way we might attempt to do this would be to examine the normal environment, or ecology, in order to discover what combinations of stimulus patterns are likely to confront the average observer—in short, to perform an *ecological survey,* which means to obtain

Figure 4-25. **Does our environment "teach" us what to see?** *Before we can either test or use the hypothesis that we see what our previous experiences have taught us to see (called empiricism; see p. 42), we have to know two things: (1) What stimulus patterns are likely to have occurred together, in frequent association, in our normal environments? (2) What is the effect of such association—if any— on what we see? One of the very few attempts to answer the first question is the study of our visual environment (called an* ecological survey*) that is summarized in (A) (Brunswik). Pictures were randomly selected from a popular magazine, and each of several depth cues (such as the cue of* vertical *position: that objects which are further away appear higher in the picture and in the optic array) was examined to measure how frequently it was associated with real distance (1), and how frequently it was "invalid" (2). Usually, we may expect the depth cues to be valid and to agree with one another, as in (B1), in which case there is little problem about what the cues will cause us to see. When cues conflict with each other, however, as in (B2), we would have to use the results of our ecological surveys (if such surveys had really been performed, which they haven't, in general) to decide which cue should prevail because it has been more frequently encountered in the normal environment—that is, we could do this if we knew also what effect the frequency of association has on the strength of perceptual learning. In the absence of both kinds of information, the empiricist hypothesis must still be regarded as speculation, not explanation.*

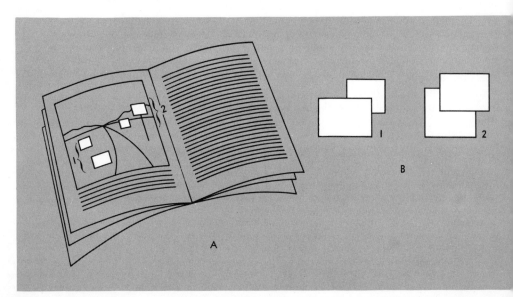

an inventory of what the world offers as raw material for the process of association (see Figure 4-25A). This is no easy task to undertake, and few ecological surveys have actually been attempted.

The task is immense. But even if we had such an ecological inventory, we could not use it directly, because now the *exact* nature of the process of perceptual learning would become critical. Consider Figure 4-25B. In 1 there is no conflict between the cue of size perspective and the cue of interposition (these cues were defined in Figure 4-3). If the two cues are set into conflict, however, as in Figure 4-25B2, how can we tell which one will prevail? If we knew that the cue of interposition had been right 1000 times and wrong 200 times in the life history of the individual, and that the cue of relative size had been right 900 times and wrong 50 times, could we say which one will predominate?

Not without more knowledge about perceptual learning: We must have precise quantitative knowledge of the laws of perceptual learning, before any ecological survey is worthwhile.

The Search for the Elements of Perceptual Learning: Physiological Models and Electronic "Perceiving Machines." Where simple receptors could be found (or imagined) to explain a particular observation, structuralists considered that observation to be an elementary sensation; otherwise, it was concluded to be a complex perception, assembled by the processes of association somewhere in the inaccessible inner recesses of the central nervous system. Donald O. Hebb has recently offered a speculative but influential hypothesis about the perceptual learning process, that is outlined in Figures 4-26 and 4-27. In essence, this theory proposes that receptor-groupings (called cell-assemblies, Figure 4-26) may develop that are sensitive to shapes, to words, to whole patterns, in just as immediate a fashion as a single color receptor was thought to be sensitive to a particular wavelength (p. 18). (These more organized units would be much more plausible than the independent sensations of Chapters 2 and 3 appear to be.)

This is really a much more complicated picture of the nervous system than any verbal discussion could evaluate. Would such a nervous system *work*? Would it learn in the same way that humans really do? The attempts to answer this question has led to the construction of perceiving machines (or simulated nervous systems) which by duplicating in electronic hardware or by a mathematical model some of the functions of particular hypothetical arrangements of neurons, seek to answer such questions. These attempts must be *preceded,* however, by perceptual research with human beings: If we design a machine to duplicate what we consider to be a particular human performance and we are wrong in our description of that performance, our machine will be irrelevant to the human nervous system in both structure and function, no matter how well it does what it was designed to do.

Perceptual Learning: Improvement and After-effects. That there are effects of learning to perceive—especially for complex patterns of stimulation—appears certain. The change in appearance of a stranger's face after he becomes a familiar friend, the sound of a foreign language (which initially sounds like gibberish) after we have learned it, the tremendous difference

63

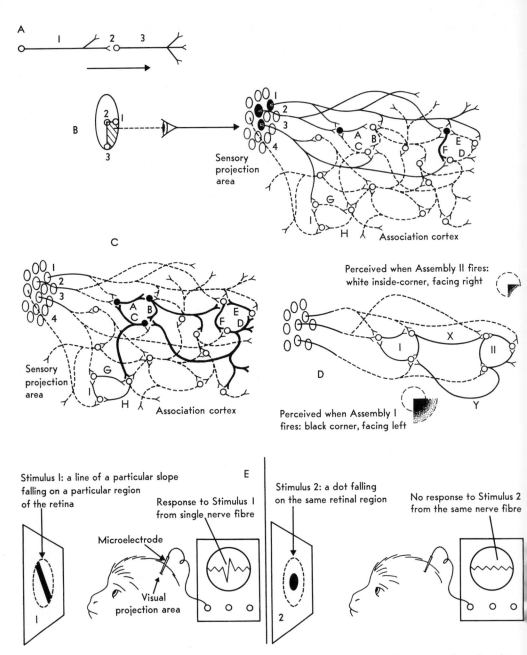

Figure 4-26. **Units of brain action: cell-assemblies and receptive fields.** *It was first thought that when any receptor neuron in a sense organ is stimulated, its activity is transmitted separately to the* sensory projection area *in the brain where it results in an elementary sensation. Elementary sensations were thought to combine into perceived objects as a result of neural processes in the* association areas *surrounding the projection areas. In this picture, the receptor processes were both the most important determinants of our perceptions, and the easiest to study. As we now know, however, individual receptor actions do not produce observable elements of experience that are simply shuffled into various combinations in the association areas. For this reason, recent years have seen a great increase in the study of (and speculation about) the brain processes that underlie sensation and perception.*

Cell-assemblies. *The neural circuitry in the cerebral cortex of the brain is immensely complex. Any attempt to explain perception in terms of cortical actions will have to use simplified analogies, or* models. *An influential example of such models is Hebb's* cell-assembly.

Let us symbolize individual nerve fibers, or neurons, as at (1) and (3), in (A). When a neuron is firing, or excited, *this excitation (which is bioelectrical in nature) is transmitted to another neuron in the direction shown by the arrow. In general, one excited neuron cannot simply excite another, but if several firing neurons have a* synapse *with an inactive one (a synapse is the point of junction (2) between two neurons), they can make it fire. Thus, neurons 1 and 2, in (B), when acting together, might fire neurons A, F, etc. In this way, the firing of particular neurons in the association cortex may depend on simultaneous stimulation by a whole* pattern *of sensory neurons.*

Some of the neurons in the association areas are set into action by stimulation of the sense organs; on the other hand, the brain includes myriad "loop circuits" (such as A, B, C in (B)), in which a number of association fibers stimulate each other. These loops are the raw material from which cell-assemblies might be carved out, by the following process.

Assume that whenever two neurons fire together, some change occurs at the synapse that strengthens the ability of the first neuron to fire the second one. Suppose that some frequently encountered pattern of stimulation on the retina (say, a corner pointing to the left) causes neurons 1, 2, and 3 to fire in the sensory cortex, and these in turn fire fibers A, B, and C in the association cortex. Since A, B, and C fire together, the connections within this loop will eventually be so strengthened that stimulating one neuron sets off a reverberating *circuit of excitation: A-B-C-A-B-C-A . . ., as shown in (C). If D, E, F is another loop which is also always fired at the same time by the same sensory event, the two loops will tend to coalesce into a single* cell-assembly, *and to fire as a unit. If either of two loops is also active by itself (without the other), however, they will remain separate assemblies that are "associated" in the sense that the firing of one loop (such as A, B, C) will increase the likelihood that the other loop (G, H, I) is fired when it is stimulated by still another source, like fiber 4, which would normally not be effective without such* facilitation *from A, B, C. Since some nerve fibers prevent others from firing, however, two cell-assemblies might* inhibit *rather than facilitate each other. Thus, if (X) and (Y) are inhibitory fibers in the arrangement at (D), either cell-assembly I or cell-assembly II would be fired by the sensory input, or they might alternate, but they could not both fire simultaneously.*

(This "flip-flop" alternation between two mutually-exclusive responses to one and the same sensory stimulus pattern characterizes the most important phenomenon in shape perception (the figure-ground phenomena discussed in pp. 58–60); without the ability to inhibit one of the two alternative shapes that are defined by the edge of each object, we should not be able to distinguish objects from the spaces between them (p. 84).)

If this description of brain function is at all valid, the smallest units of perception would be the result of firing these cell-assemblies, rather than the firing of specific receptor neurons. Each such cell-assembly would correspond to a simple common unit of sensory stimulation, such as a corner or a particular slope of a line in vision, a vowel sound in hearing, a pressure-pattern in touch. Whether or not such cell-assemblies do develop in the association areas, very similiar units of complex neural action have been found in the sensory projection areas themselves.

Receptive fields. *With very fine wires, called* microelectrodes, *the excitation of single neurons has been recorded from within the visual projection areas of various animals, and neurons have been discovered through this technique that fire when some particular pattern (such as a line or an edge of a particular slope) stimulates an entire* field *of retinal receptors, and that do not fire when individual rods or cones are stimulated by points of light in the same retinal area (E) (Hubel and Wiesel). Unlike cell-assemblies, these line-sensitive and edge-sensitive cells are found in the sensory projection system. Like the cell-assemblies, they offer us a fresh approach to the study of sensory psychophysics, using much larger units of analysis (such as lines, corners, and edges of about $\frac{1}{4}°$ by 4 to 8 degrees of visual angle in size) than those with which we first started— the specific nerve energies of punctiform receptor action.*

Although these units of response are larger and more complex than those of traditional sensory psychophysics, they are still only fragments of the things we see. How might these cell-assemblies and receptive fields combine to form the objects and events of normal perception? Hebb's speculative sketch of this process is called the phase sequence, *a version of which we shall consider briefly in Figure 4-27.*

Figure 4-27. **The organization of cell-assemblies into phase sequences.** *When we look at an object, such as the silhouette of a vase in (A), our gaze shifts from one* fixation *to another (say from F_0 to F_1 to F_2, etc.) and different sets of cell-assemblies will be stimulated as different patterns of stimulation—S_0, S_1, and S_2—fall on the fovea of the eye. Consider the first moment in time, T_0: with fixation F_0, the pattern of stimulation, S_0, facilitates the firing of cell-assemblies C_1 and Y_1 (to consider just two of many). If it were actually fired, C_1 might be experienced as "black-corner-pointing-left," while Y_1 might be "white-inside-corner-facing-right." (These two alternatives might well be mutually inhibitory, as shown in Figure 4-26E, in accordance with what we know about figure-ground perception (p. 84).)*

Which cell-assembly, C_1 or Y_1, would fire? Which shape would be seen?

At moment T_0, the brain will not, of course, be idle: Reverberations will be continuing from the previous moment's visual (or nonvisual) sensory stimulation, and from whatever cell-assemblies had just been firing before S_0 fell on the eye. Let C_0 represent all the cell-assemblies that happen to be active at T_0. Their firing will facilitate the firing of other cell-assemblies, as we saw in Figure 4-26D. Suppose that C_1 and X_1 are the cell-assemblies that C_0 would facilitate. Of the three possible sets of outcomes (X_1, Y_1, and C_1), only C_1 would receive sufficient converging excitation to be fired and, in consequence, the observer would perceive a "black-corner-pointing-left."

Similarly, at the next fixation, F_1, the new pattern of stimulation falling on the fovea of the eye might facilitate two cell-assemblies (among others): C_2 ("black-inside-corner-facing-left") and Y_2 ("white-corner-pointing-right"). At this moment, T_1, C_1 will just have been fired by the events described above. If C_1 facilitates C_2 rather than Y_2—that is, if the observer "expects" C_2—the momentary pattern of stimulation (S_1) and the ongoing cortical processes (C_1) will both combine to produce the perception of "black-inside-corner-facing-left" at fixation F_1. As the observer continues to scan the object, the cortical processes set up by successive fixations will select the cell-assemblies to be seen at later fixations, and a smooth and consistent sequence of these elementary edges and corners will constitute the perception of the entire object—in this case, a black vase.

This description of a sequence of selection of alternative cell-assemblies (see Hebb) is plausible in broad outline, but it is still too vague to make usable predictions about how objects will be perceived. Most particularly, it makes no provision for a very important principle that appears to govern this process of selection, the minimum principle, *which we shall discuss in the next chapter (pp. 87–94).*

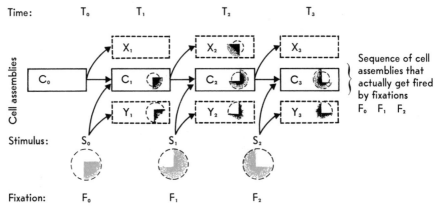

between the appearance of a map or a circuit diagram before and after we have learned about such matters—all of these seem to guarantee that such effects exist (see Figure 4-28E).

There are many different kinds of perceptual change that can be demonstrated and a number of these that have been the subject of particularly vigorous research are surveyed in Figure 4-28. Few even resemble a simple process of association at all closely, and none of them offer the kind of knowledge about perceptual learning that would be needed to make the empiricist theory more than a vague hypothesis.

What can we conclude about the empiricist theory of perception?

THE REMAINS OF THE NATURE-NURTURE DEBATE

Many of the issues raised by the structuralist enterprise remain active today. In most cases, their importance used to rest on a theoretical structure which, as we have seen, is now quite discredited. In consequence, though this is not always recognized, these questions are today quite different from their original formulations. The controversy about empiricism is a good example of this.

Do we see space (or shape, or direction) innately, or are such perceptual abilities learned, as the empiricist argument maintains? At first glance, one might think that the question would be simply settled. On the contrary, it entails extreme subtleties, and almost any sweeping statement made about the relative contributions of nature and nurture today is bound to be premature and irresponsible.

But this in itself tells us something about the problem. If the two alternatives offered clearly different predictions about perceptual abilities, or about the extent to which those abilities are educable or modifiable, they would be simple enough to separate and test. If, for example, the existence of an innate basis for space perception meant that perception would be fixed and unmodifiable, or if a learned basis for perception meant that it would be modifiable or educable (so that we could raise different people to perceive in different ways), then we would also, by the same token, have the basis for distinguishing between these two alternatives. Unfortunately, the issue is not so clearcut. It is perfectly possible that perceptual learning occurs in very early infancy, and resists further modification or relearning; at the other extreme, we might be born with a full set of perceptual abilities that are, although innate, subject to continual change and education. With this in mind, the difficulty of deciding the nature-nurture issue becomes evident. But a further question then comes to the fore. If no such clear-cut alternatives attend either a nature or a nurture picture of perceptual development, under what conditions does this become an important issue?

Western tradition and common sense both incline toward an empiricist view. What conceivable innate mechanisms could explain space perception? Isn't it easier to imagine that this ability is learned? Not necessarily. Whatever the effects of learning may be, they must consist of changes in the nervous system, so that after the learning has occurred, the nervous system has a particular wiring, or set of interconnections. There is no reason why, as a result

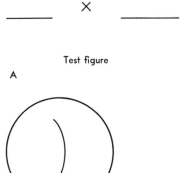

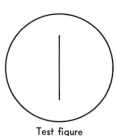

Test figure   Inspection figure

A

Inspection figure   Test figure

2

Figure 4-28. Recent research in perceptual change. Several varieties of perceptual change are currently receiving a great deal of attention, partly because they seem to offer the hope of coming to grips with the fundamental problem of perceptual learning.

(A) Adaptation, after-effects, and successive contrasts. *The prolonged viewing of any color produces an afterimage of the opposite hue (p. 23). Such effects are usually attributed to fatigue: fatigue of the specific color receptors that had been stimulated, so that the remaining color receptors, being fresh and unfatigued, contribute disproportionately to what we see. Yet similar after-effects of prolonged viewing can be demonstrated for such complex properties as visual size (1), shape (2), and motion (3), and for location in haptic space (the space we know through our sense of touch). Does this imply that there are specific receptors that are responsible for these perceptions?*

(1) **Figural after-effects.** *At left is a test figure. When you fixate point ×, the sets of parallel lines should appear to be equally separated. At right is an inspection figure. Fixate × in the inspection figure steadily for about 60 seconds, and then return to the test figure. The separation will usually now appear to be greater between the right-hand set of parallel lines. These results suggest that contours are repelled from regions that were previously satiated by other contours. The effect is restricted to the satiated region, increasing up to a maximum, and then decreasing again as the test figure is moved away from the satiated zone (W. Köhler and Wallach).*

(2) **Shape after-effects.** *At right is a test-figure, at left an inspection figure. If you make a tube or reduction screen that will restrict your vision to the lines themselves, and run your eye up and down the inspection figure for about 60 seconds, when you then fixate the test figure, it will appear to curve in the*

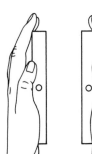
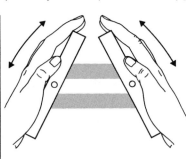
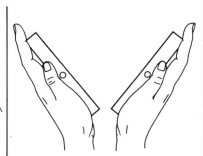

Test objects, set to parallel, before "satiation" Inspection object over which hands are moved Test objects set to apparent parallel after "satiation"

3

opposite direction. What was initially curved now looks less so, and what was initially straight now looks curved. Similar shifts will occur if the inspection figure is a tilted line, an angled line, and so on. In each case, the test figure will appear changed in the direction opposite to that in which the inspection figure differed from it (Gibson).

A single mechanism will probably not explain all these visual after-effects, since the contour-repulsion explanation depends on fixation (and in fact can be obtained in the complete absence of eye-movements (Krausskopf)), whereas the shape-contrast phenomena occur with free eye-movement, and some varieties actually require voluntary bodily movements by the observer in order to occur (see below). Furthermore, there are very similar after-effects that depend on motion by their very nature (see B), in which a contour-repulsion explanation therefore seems completely inapplicable.

(3) **Kinesthetic and proprioceptive after-effects.** *Even more dramatic after-effects occur in the tactual-kinesthetic perception of shape and position. A blindfolded observer who rubs his hands back and forth across the inspection object obtains an astonishingly large after-effect when he then adjusts two testboards between his hands so that they feel parallel. These after-effects can certainly not be attributed to any conceivable set of sensory receptor neurons, since whole muscle systems are involved. Instead, the after-effects occur in a space that transcends the individual tactual receptors and kinesthetic receptors which are stimulated during the inspection period (Gibson and Backlund). This is called haptic space, the space we learn about by touch, kinesthesis, and proprioception (see Figure 4-9).*

(B) **Changed relationships between the sensory modalities.** *The relationship between different modalities, such as vision and kinesthesis, readily changes with practice or adaptation. The relationship between visual up and down, and the "meanings" of these visual observations with respect to the body image (p. 44), can be at least partially upset and relearned—for example, by wearing inverting spectacles. Within the course of a couple of weeks, the observer can even ride a bicycle; after removing the glasses, the world now "looks upside down" for a while. Some of these visuomotor adaptations are dramatic, and clearly involve changes in vision itself; after adapting to spectacles with split-color lenses, the world looks yellow when you look to the left, and blue when you look to the right . . . after you remove the spectacles (I. Kohler).*

These changes in relationship between vision and the body image require co-ordinated action and vision in order to occur. An observer wearing distorting spectacles will obtain no adaptation while watching his hand move, passively, or while being wheeled around in space (Mikaelian and Held). To what extent these are changes within vision itself, and to what extent these effects are due to alteration of the body image alone (see Figure 4-9), are questions that are not yet answered. In any case, these phenomena are the closest approach to anything like a process of association in perceptual learning.

(C) **Selective recognition of alternative "organizations."** *Many situations are ambiguous, in that we can observe several quite different shapes. Our previous experi-*

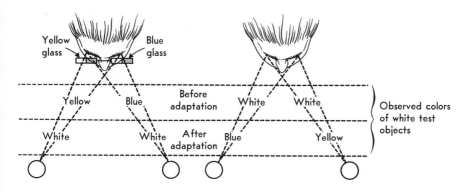

C

 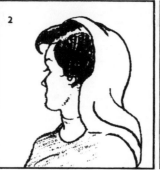 

ences can influence which alternative we do perceive: At (1) we see a young lady in profile, at (3) an old woman. Subjects who had previously seen (1) can at first only see (2) as a young lady; similarly, those who had first seen (3) could only see (2) as an old lady (Leeper). We shall see in Chapter 6 that these procedures have also been used to study the effects of motives and rewards on perceiving.

(D) **Changes in recognition thresholds.** If we use light that is too weak, or exposure times that are too short, or use out-of-focus slide projectors, the patterns or words that we show a subject will be undiscernible. By gradually increasing the light intensity or the exposure duration, or by improving the focus of the projector, we will reach a point at which the patterns can be recognized, that is, we will have a recognition threshold than can be measured by the psychophysical methods (p. 8). Practice, familiarity, and the observer's expectations (and, perhaps, his conscious and unconscious desires as well) appear to affect these recognition thresholds. Thus, the mirror images of letters (1) require longer exposures in order to be correctly reported than do the images in (2) which are normally oriented letters (Henle). It is not yet known whether such differences are merely response biases (see p. 8) due to lower readiness to say the names of the letters in the case of reversed stimuli, since thresholds for judging whether two patterns are "same" or "different," as in (3) and (4), are no higher for reversed or for rarely used letters than for normal and frequently used ones (Hayes, Robinson, and Brown).

There is no doubt that the effects of past experience have been amply shown to affect the recognition and report of the learned names and meanings of letters, words, and shapes. If we wish to draw conclusions from such research about the underlying processes of shape perception, however, the question becomes a much trickier one, and no satisfactory evidence supports such effects. We cannot use measures of perception that themselves depend on learning, if we are trying to demonstrate the effects of learning on perception.

(E) **Arabic scribbles and distinctive features.** One effect of practice and experience may be to increase the differentiation in what we perceive, that is, to enable us to see distinguishing characteristics and distinctive features by which we can respond differently to stimuli that previously looked all alike. In the demonstration given here (after Gibson and Gibson), the row of curlicues running across the page at (1) has a row of names beneath it. Study the row carefully, trying to learn the name that goes with each scribble. The next row, (2) is a scrambled set of the same curlicues. Without looking at the first set, try to name the items in the second set, and then check yourself. How many errors did you make? Finally, without going back to row (1) turn the book with the right-hand edge on the bottom so that the set of curlicues runs vertically; again, try to name them. How many fewer errors did you have the second time? If you had fewer errors the second time, to what factors can you attribute the difference?

D

1   2   3   4

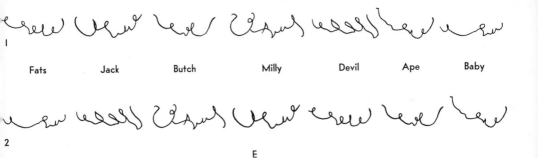

1							
Fats	Jack	Butch	Milly	Devil	Ape	Baby

2

E

of millions of years of evolution, the individual cannot be born "prewired," that is, born with whatever connections are necessary to perceive tridimensional space when presented with the appropriate stimulation. We will discuss one of such possible mechanisms later (p. 88).

The fact is this: that one can find empiricist "explanations" of almost any perceptual phenomenon, at our present state of knowledge—even explanations of two mutually exclusive outcomes (see p. 62). If the same theory predicts that one object, A, will look nearer than another, B, and it also predicts the reverse, we really can't use the theory. Such explanations are useless for predicting what we will perceive in any specific situation, as well as invulnerable to refutation.

The problem is no longer a broad, philosophical issue, inviting amateur opinion. Instead, it has become a tangled, technical question which is interesting mainly to physiologists and to students of growth and development. It is certainly no longer *the* central issue in the study of perception as such.

ALTERNATIVES TO STRUCTURALISM

We have come to the end of any consistent attempt to build up the perceived world out of simple sensations that correspond to simple elementary physical variables. Next we will try "higher" units of analysis: *figures, edges, angles, and surfaces,* both stationary and in motion. Whether some of these are innately "prewired," or are put together in infancy by the formation of of cell-assemblies (Fig. 4-26), is still very much an open question.

SUMMARY

In this chapter, we applied what we know about the appearances of very simple stimuli to the perception of more normal and more complicated happenings.

Thus, in Chapter 3, the unit of visual response seemed to be the sensation of a point of light, whose apparent color and position depends on the stimulus and on where the stimulus triggers some retinal receptor. Normally, of course, the scene we face stimulates many thousands of retinal receptors; does what we see, then, consist only of the aggregate of the sensations produced by those receptors, only of a two-dimensional mosaic that varies in its

Perceiving
Objects
as Structures
of Sensations

hue, saturation and brightness from one region to the next? Don't we also see shapes, distances, motions, facial expressions?

The answer explored in this chapter is that in fact we don't *see* shapes, distances, or motions, at all: that we only *see* points of colored light in various arrangements, but that some of these arrangements have the memories of *nonvisual* sensations strongly associated with them. According to this theory, when we look at an object—say, an apple—what we actually see is only a red patch: If the apple is near, the red patch is large, and we remember that our hand need only reach out to touch it; if the apple is far, the patch is small, and we remember that our legs had to make some number of steps before our hand would touch it. The size of the red patch has thus become a visual "cue" that brings to mind those memories of reaching and walking that comprise the apparent depth or distance of the apple. Of course, there are many other depth cues beside size (such as perspective, binocular disparity), and there are many other kinds of nonvisual memories that might be aroused by the visual sensations (the apple's tart taste, its smooth feel, and so on), but the basic theory (structuralism) has been illustrated. The multitude of different things and happenings we perceive are simply composed of the sensations and of the memories of previous sensations.

If we could accept this structuralist theory wholeheartedly, the study of perception would rest directly on a set of fundamental elements, the sensations that are discovered by the procedures of sensory psychophysics; this in turn would give a clear purpose to those procedures, to the studies of simple stimuli.

Unfortunately, it is easy to show that complex stimuli do not appear as we would expect them to be perceived from the ways in which their parts appear. The same patch of light that is one color when viewed separately, looks very different when it is surrounded by light of another color. Similarly for shapes, sizes, motions: All frequently appear quite different from what we should expect from this theory. These differences may be classed under various headings (such as the Perceptual Constancies, the Illusions, and the effects of Organization), but they all add up to this: that what we have learned from sensory psychophysics will enable us to predict with assurance how only the very simplest stimuli are perceived.

The study of our sensory responses to simple stimuli does not, therefore, give us wholly satisfactory units with which to analyze our perceptions of more complex objects and events. We shall examine alternative approaches in the next two chapters.

Higher-Order Variables

in Perception

In Chapter 3 we saw that the physical stimulation which reaches our sensory organs from the objects and events around us can be completely analyzed into a relatively small number of elementary physical variables, and that these local stimulus variables appeared to produce correspondingly elementary sensations (or simple observations). In Chapter 4 we saw that many problems arise when we attempt to use this knowledge to predict how entire objects (instead of elementary physical variables) are observed. The classical remedy was to invoke our past experiences to explain these discrepancies. This complication is frequently unnecessary as we shall see.

73

5

Whenever observers agree about what they see, the following must be true. No matter how complicated the stimulus is, and no matter how great the effects of past experiences (and of other unknown factors), *there must be some discoverable psychophysical relationship between the objects viewed and the perceptions that result.* If there were nothing in the stimulus pattern to govern the response, there obviously could be no agreement (except by chance) among observers. If combining two stimuli changes their appearance, then there must be something about the combination itself which elicits that change. That is, in addition to the local physical characteristics of each stimulus, the *relationship between them* may be an important variable. A relationship that exists between individual measures is called a *higher-order variable.* Let us see whether higher-order variables can be discovered that will account for the discrepancies of color, size, and form—the constancies and illusions and organizations which we encountered in Chapter 4.

Color

Vary the intensity of a single patch of light, and its lightness changes; keep its intensity constant, but vary that of a ring surrounding it, and its lightness again changes. Evidently the stimulus variables that determine the lightnesses of adjacent regions of light are not simply their intensities; some relationship *between* the regions must be considered as well. What is the simplest relationship between the intensities of two regions that suggests itself as the higher-order variable which might account for the apparent lightnesses of those regions? Let's try *ratios* of intensities (see Figure 5-1). If the apparent lightness of a region— say, the disc marked ? in part A—is proportional to *the ratio between its intensity and that of its surrounding region,* instead of simply being proportional to its intensity, the two inner discs should appear of equal lightness when ? = 50 mL. In fact, that is what happens. The lightness constancy and contrast phenomena discussed in pp. 51–55 seem simple to understand in these terms.

In general, simple *ratios* of stimulation will predict what we see far better than will measures of the patches considered separately.

Even so, we cannot merely replace the simple addition hypothesis by an equally simple ratio hypothesis. As the complexity of the stimulus pattern increases, the prediction of the perceived lightness of any region becomes more difficult (Figure 5-1B). There is also a hint of potential trouble to be found in Figure 5-1C, for even though the ratios of stimulation must remain unchanged (since the stimulation itself remains unchanged), the lightness of the surfaces we see appears to depend on how we "interpret" the *spatial* arrangements. The hue of any region also turns out to depend on the wavelength of its surroundings as well as upon its own wavelength (Figure 5-2): This suggests very strongly that the prediction of hue, like that of lightness, will prove to require stimulus measures based on the relationship between regions, rather than on the stimulation within any region.

Higher-Order
Variables
in Perception

74

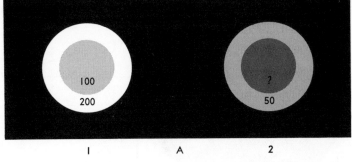

Figure 5-1. Relative intensities and relative whiteness. (A) On the left, disc (1) set at 100 mL (millilamberts, which are units of light-energy, or luminance); on the right, disc (2), with variable luminance. Each disc is surrounded by a ring of light in an otherwise dark room. The ring around disc (1) is kept at 200 mL; the ring around disc (2) is set at 50 mL. At what setting will disc (2) look exactly as white as disc (1)? Not at 100 mL, but at 25 mL! The two discs are certainly not equal in physical luminance at that setting; in what way are they equal? The discs appear equally white when the ratio of surround-luminance to disc-luminance is equal for each disc. Thus, if we increase the luminance of disc (2) as shown on the horizontal axis of graph (B), but are careful to increase the luminance of the surround at the same rate so that the ratio of surround-luminance to disc-luminance is kept constant (the straight line A in graph (B)), the whiteness of disc (2) also remains constant and equal to the whiteness of disc (1) (Wallach).

If we now assume that the stimulus variable which determines perceived whiteness is not the absolute amount of light-energy at all, but is instead the ratio of light-energy of adjacent regions in the field of view, the phenomenon of lightness constancy (p. 50) becomes considerably easier to understand, since the ratio of intensities of light reaching the eye from each of several objects is in fact constant, regardless of changes in the illumination, as long as the reflectance of each object remains constant (see Figure 4-15).

(B) Although we can thus tell better how white an object will look by considering the ratio of its neighboring regions' luminances to its own than by considering its absolute level of luminance, this simple ratio is itself only successful for certain ranges of luminance. For different luminances (and for different arrangements of the lighted regions), maintaining a constant ratio of luminances for disc and surround no longer assures us that the appearance of disc (2) will remain constant (as shown by lines B and C in the graph) (Hess and Pretori; Jameson and Hurvich). Because of these inadequacies of the simple ratio hypothesis, Jameson and Hurvich argue for a different relationship between luminance and whiteness. They propose a white/ black opponent-processes pair of receptors similar to the red/green and yellow/ blue pairs we discussed in Figure 3-10 (p. 23) and a scheme which should account for whiteness constancy as well as for color contrast (p. 55): The whiteness response in any part of the visual field

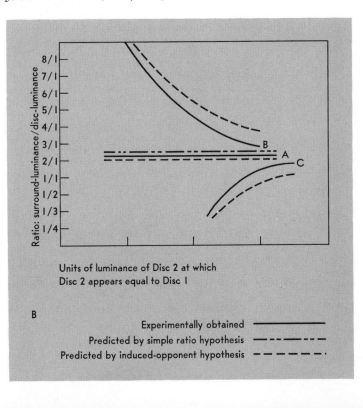

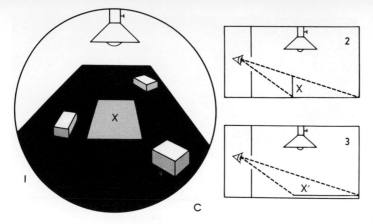

such as disc (2) would be the sum of two components: a direct component, which is the effect of the stimulus energy falling on that region of the retina, and an indirect or induced effect, which is proportional to the amount of the whiteness response in the surround, but is opposite in sign (that is, the induced response is black if the surrounding regions are white, and vice versa).

As the dotted lines in the graph show, the equations that are based on this proposal (see next paragraph) fit the results of whiteness-matching experiments quite well.

If R_i is the over-all whiteness response in disc (1), it would depend on the luminance of the disc, S_i, and on the response, R_s, in the surrounding ring:

$$R_i = (S_i)^{\frac{1}{3}} - k(R_s)$$

Similarly, the response in the surround, R_s, would depend on the luminance of the surround, S_s, and the amount of the response in the disc:

$$R_s = (S_s)^{\frac{1}{3}} - k(R_i)$$

The constant, k, determines how much the surround affects the apparent whiteness of the disc (and vice versa), and this value decreases as the distance between the interacting regions increases.

(C) Can we really account for our perceptions of whiteness completely in terms of relative luminances alone, as our discussions in both (A) and (B) suggest? No: If we change the apparent orientation of a surface to the source of its illumination, the apparent whiteness of the surface changes also, even though the light-energy entering the eye remains unchanged! Object X in the view at (1) may look like an upright trapezoid in glancing illumination, which it really is (2), or it may look like a horizontal square receiving full illumination (3). If it is caused to change its apparent spatial orientation from (3) to (2) (for example, by waving a stick behind X), it becomes darker in appearance, even though the actual light reaching the eye has not changed (Hochberg and Beck). You may observe the same phenomenon by staring at an unevenly lit corner of the room you are in, and "forcing it" to appear flat—something you will be able to do with a little effort. What happens to the relative lightness of the two walls when you do this?

This phenomenon seems very much like the result of some "unconscious inference" (in which you calculate how bright an object is by taking into account its apparent slant-toward-the-light and, hence, the illumination it appears to receive). The apparent whiteness does not vary predictably with the actual degree of slant, however, as it should were unconscious inference the basis of the phenomenon, and a systematic explanation for this class of effects has not yet been found.

Absolute, Relative, and Familiar Size

With only one patch of stimulation on the retina of the eye, only one basis for a size-response exists: the size of the retinal image (or the visual angle subtended at the eye, Figure 3-3). This is called the *absolute size* of the stimulus. With more stimuli, a higher-order variable appears—the ratio of the size of one image on the retina relative to the sizes of the other images. This is called the *relative size* of the stimulus. The structuralist approach assumed that our nervous systems are responsive to the absolute sizes of the retinal images, and that any departure from this simple relationship is to be explained either by our knowledge about the real size, gained through our familiarity with the object, or by our calculations which take the object's distance into account.

As we saw in Figure 3-3 and on p. 56, there is a simple trigonometric relationship between size and distance. For a given size of visual angle, if the absolute size of the image is measured by angle θ, then $\tan \theta = S/D$, where S = the physical size of the object itself, and D = the object's distance. If we know the visual angle, or absolute size, and the distance of the object, we might calculate its physical objective size. Conversely, if we know the visual angle, or absolute size, and are familiar with the object's physical size, we might calculate its distance.

This introduces still another term: *familiar size.* In terms of Berkeley's original assumption, every familiar object is considered to have some *assumed* or familiar distal size, which has been obtained by previous knowledge of the

Figure 5-2. Colored shadows and "full-color" pictures from "one color." (A) Light of 650 millimicron wavelength is red in hue (p. 21); light of 530 mμ appears green. A shadow (3) cast by such red-hued light of 650 mμ (1) looks green, even though no light of 530 mμ is present. The apparent hue of the shadow region (3) is determined by its relationship to the surrounding "red" region (2), not to the absolute wavelength of the light coming from the shadow itself, and simultaneous color contrast, or induction, occurs (see p. 55). (B) If a slide of colored objects, photographed through a red filter, is projected on a screen in red-hued light (650

mμ), and another slide, photographed through a green filter, is projected in precise superposition in white (unfiltered) light, greens, blues, and yellows appear on the screen, as well as reds (Land). Can you explain why the green appears? How about yellow? blue? orange? (see p. 23).

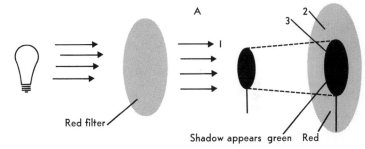

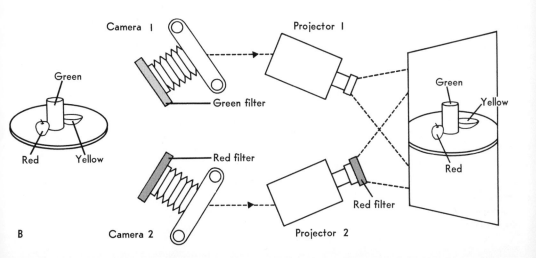

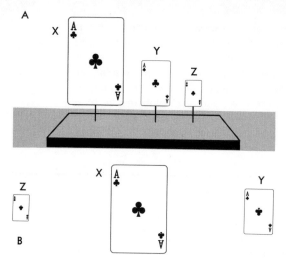

Figure 5-3. Familiar size. (A) Only Y is a normal playing card; X is twice normal size; Z is half normal size. All are at the same distance from the observer, but the base is hidden by the screen. Viewing all the cards at once monocularly, observers judge X to be nearest and Z furthest, with Y appearing halfway between (Ittelson and Kilpatrick). Does this imply that we perceive each card to be normal size, and distribute them in apparent space in ways that will be consistent with their retinal sizes? Consider the next experiment. (B) Viewed one at a time, the cards yield no consistent differences as to the distances at which they are judged to be (Gogel, Hartman, and Harker; Epstein et al.). What other distance cues might have been working in (A) that are not present in (B)?

object. Does this familiar size both tell us the size of the object the next time we see it, and, taken in conjunction with the absolute retinal size, allow us to calculate its distance unconsciously?

One experiment which is frequently quoted in support of familiar size is shown in Figure 5-3. Observers were required to estimate the distance of a normal playing card (Y), one which was twice normal size (X), and one which was half normal size (Z). In the absence of any other distance cues, the estimated distances were found to be appropriate to the cards' sizes: X seemed at half Y's distance, Z seemed at twice Y's distance. Does this clearly demonstrate the operation of the familiar size cues? Not at all.

This experiment fails completely to separate the proposed operation of familiar size from a strong higher-order variable, that of relative size (or ratio of the images' sizes). If we attempt to separate the two, relative size can easily be shown to operate, whereas familiar size has not yet been shown effective (Figure 5-4). If we repeat the playing-card experiment but *with only one card present at a time,* relative size, as a distance cue, is removed, and only familiar size remains to produce differences in apparent distances of the cards —if it can. And it cannot, apparently, for there are no systematic differences in the apparent distances of the cards (Figure 5-3B). One final experiment discredits the simple absolute-size hypothesis directly. Observers are instructed to set a variable stimulus (V), which is viewed under natural conditions, equal to a standard (S), which is viewed monocularly in complete darkness (Figure 5-5); *they are simply incapable of setting V so that the retinal sizes match.*

Neither absolute nor familiar size seem to be of great importance for the observation of either size *or* distance. One interesting proposal appears in Figure 5-6. In a normal environment, our size judgments are made about *objects on a surface,* not for points in empty space. The surface on which the objects stand is likely to be covered with a reasonably uniform pattern, or *texture.* If we take the number of elements of texture covered or obscured by an object, i, to be T_i, and the number covered by object, ii, to be T_{ii}, then

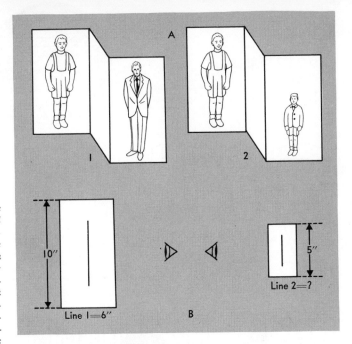

Figure 5-4. Relative size and size-ratios. (A) At (1), the man and boy are the same relative sizes and the same retinal sizes, but different familiar sizes (that is, the familiar size of a man is about six feet, and of a boy about three feet); at (2), both boys have the same familiar size, but different relative sizes. In which pair is there a more pronounced and stable depth-difference? When all relevant factors (for instance, left vs. right) are controlled, the difference in depth between the two sides is strong at (2), and absent or weak at (1). What does this suggest concerning the experiment in Figure 5-3A? (B) This experiment is directly analogous to that in Figure 5-1A. In an otherwise dark room, an observer first views the standard line (1) (say, six inches in length), then judges whether the variable line (2) appears to be of equal length. The two lines are judged to be equal when line 2 is approximately three inches long (Rock and Ebenholtz). To what variable of stimulation does this judgment correspond?

the ratio of these two numbers, T_i/T_{ii}, provides a higher-order variable of stimulation that should usually be in perfect correspondence with the actual physical sizes of the objects. That is, *it is possible to find variables of stimu-*

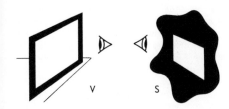

Figure 5-5. Can we observe retinal size at all? Observers attempt to match the image size of a normally viewed variable (V) to a standard that is viewed without any distance cues (that is, viewed monocularly and in an otherwise dark room). They are simply unable to make a match (Wallach and McKenna). If observers cannot detect retinal size, can familiar size be an effective distance cue? (See p. 56.)

Figure 5-6. What is constant in size constancy? Surfaces usually have reasonably uniform textures; that is, the average size of the surface irregularities of the surface is the same from one region to another. If the stimulus variable upon which we base our judgments about the size of an object were the number of texture elements it covers, we would have at least one explanation for the phenomena of size constancy (p. 51), since this variable will remain constant for a given distal object size, regardless of the distance from which the object is viewed (Gibson).

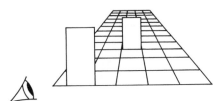

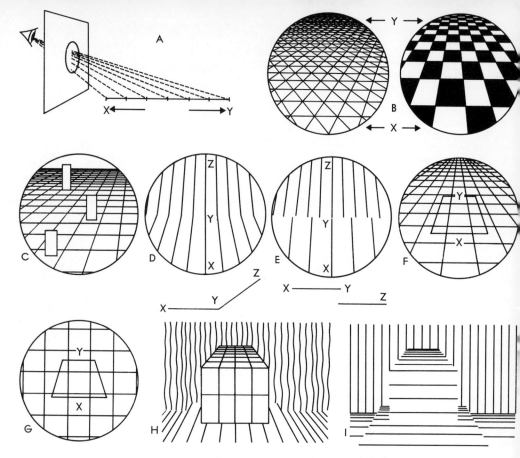

Figure 5-7. Texture-density gradients as informative variables of stimulation. *In (A) we see why a uniform texture on the ground produces a texture-density gradient at the eye, and, although the texture may vary (B), the gradient itself remains the same for a given degree of slant. These gradients of texture-density carry information about the sizes of objects (familiar or otherwise) standing on the surface (C), and, in addition, they carry information about the arrangement of surfaces with respect to each other. In (D) we see how an abrupt change in gradient results in an apparent dihedral angle (that is, an angle between surfaces); in (E), an edge or drop between parallel surfaces is indicated by a change in density and a constant gradient. Even shape constancy (see Figure 4-14B) might be accounted for in these terms. In (F) the rear edge (Y) of the geometrical figure is the same number of texture-units wide as is the front edge (X), so that the figure can serve as a stimulus for "square-at-a-slant"; in (G), on the other hand, (Y) is a smaller number of texture-units wide than is (X), and the texture gradient itself is zero (signifying "no slant"), so that the figure is the stimulus for "trapezoid-in-frontal-parallel." In all these illustrations (after Gibson, 1950), the gradient is the unit of analysis, not the points of light and dark of which any particular example is composed; thus, we could replace any or all of the surfaces in (H) by a quite different pattern (as in I), yet leave both the gradients and the apparent spatial arrangements of the scene unchanged. In (J), these sources of information about space are not used as fully as they might be. If they were, we would perceive the world of distal stimuli veridically (that is, our perceptions of angles, sizes, distances, and so forth, would all be perfect). This is simply not always true: Observers who are asked to set (X) so that it is parallel to (Y) in (1), choose a setting approximately at (X'), which is more in accordance with what is present in the optic array at (1') than it is with the true distal arrangement, at (1) (O. W. and P. C. Smith).*

lation that automatically take distance into account, if we accept the possibility of ratios as being stimuli to which the nervous system can respond. In fact, if we take one step beyond the *ratio* as a higher-order variable, we obtain a revolutionary new picture of the information that is available to our senses—although we don't know yet to what extent they can use that information.

Gradients as Potential Stimuli:
Toward a Psychophysics of Surfaces

A stimulus ratio measures the rate at which some variable changes between two regions on the sensory surface. It is appropriate to *pairs* of stimuli. The physical world, however, is not really characterized by pairs of regions (which is what we have been talking about so far in this section) any more than by individual points (which is what we discussed in Chapters 2 and 3). We are usually confronted by continuous surfaces, by extended objects, by prolonged motions. The rate at which some measured property changes over a continuous, extended stimulus is called a *gradient*.

From Berkeley on, most philosophers, physiologists, and psychologists had started with the assumption that we cannot account for our perceptions of space in terms of the information in visual stimulation, and had gone on from there to try to discover how we made up for this inadequacy. The first real challenge to this tradition came from James J. Gibson, who started with the inescapable fact that people *do* perceive space, and concluded, therefore, that some kind of information *must* be present in visual stimulation. The *gradient of texture density* is a particularly promising higher-order variable for this purpose. If you look straight ahead at a homogeneously textured surface, the density of the texture does not change from one part of the optic array to the next, so that the gradient of texture-density is zero; as the slant increases, the density of texture changes from the near edge to the far edge, and the gradient, or rate of change, increases. Figure 5-7 shows several ways in which the gradient of texture-density could provide the observer with precise and relatively unambiguous information about the distances, sizes, and slants of the surfaces and objects in the world.

The examples of Figure 5-7 provide an impressive analytical vocabulary.

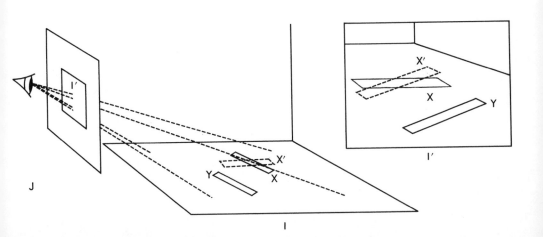

By assembling the proper texture-density gradients we can produce almost any collection of objects and surfaces. With texture gradients as the physical stimulus variables, and perceived surface slant as the psychological unit, we *may* have *a new set of elements with which to undertake the analysis of our perceptions of the physical world.*

We cannot overestimate the importance of these variables, if they do in fact account for the constancies, for several reasons: Compared to anything we have encountered until now, they offer a very different kind of analysis, they require a different picture of the physiological processes involved, and they set a different group of tasks for the psychologist. If an observer's ability to use these higher-order variables is the result of learning at all, it is quite a different kind of learning from the association of images with tactual-kinesthetic memories.

Despite its great promise, however, this approach is still in its infancy, and certain cautions are in order. (1) It is still largely programmatic; we don't know, for example, what surface angles will be perceived when specific gradients are combined—that is, both the analytic units and the laws of their combination are in need of quantitative psychophysical study. (2) The explanation is *too* good, for it provides the observer with enough information for the constancies to be complete and for our space perception to be perfect, and neither of these is true (see Figure 5-7J). We have to know whether we actually *use* these potentially informative stimulus variables before we can consider them to be explanations of the constancies. (3) Surfaces have important qualities in addition to their slants, and these will require quite different kinds of analysis. For example, they may vary from *rough* to *smooth,* from *matte* to *glossy.* (4) No specific physiological bases, whether innate or acquired, have yet been proposed that would account for these higher-order variables as elementary processes in the nervous system. (5) Finally, "shape" itself has been left out. Nothing in our description of a texture-density-gradient allows us to distinguish a square from a circle, a smile from a frown.

We have considered all the physical attributes of a perceived stationary object but one—its shape, or form—and this is the most important and challenging of all. What can the higher-order variables be that decide what form will be observed? Before we attempt to apply perceptual psychophysical procedures to the study of form, let us return to the successor to structuralism, *Gestalt* theory, which was concerned above all else with this problem.

THE GESTALTIST LAWS OF ORGANIZATION

In *Gestalt* theory, the first serious attempt to deal with perception as other than an assemblage of independent point sensations, there were two interwoven programs for research. The first (which is still in progress) was to find natural units of analysis of perception with which to replace the artificial sensations; the other was to explain these new units in terms of a totally revised picture of how the nervous system works. These programs were launched by Max Wertheimer in the 1920's; under the leadership of Wertheimer, Kurt Koffka, and Wolfgang Köhler, *Gestalt* theory dominated the study of perception during the next two decades.

The Gestaltists' general aim was to re-analyze our perception of the world. *Gestalt* means "whole," "configuration," or "form," and the *Gestalt* position was itself something of a *Gestalt,* whose argument really makes sense only after you have gone all the way through it twice. The *Gestalt* criticisms of structuralism run as follows.

A percept is *not* composed of sensations. "Sensations" are artificial kinds of perception that appear only under the special conditions of the physiological and psychological laboratories. Sensations are *not* elementary experiences, and consequently all the speculations about independent receptors, and about individual specific nerve energies, are in error. For these reasons, the precise measurement techniques of sensory psychophysics are likely to be irrelevant until we first discover what it is we should measure, and those of analytic introspection are utterly invalid. What then should we do instead?

If we take a new look at the world of perception, unbiased by any structuralist assumptions, what do we find as the most natural units of analysis? In the world of sight—not meaningless tiny patches of light and color, but whole shaped regions, set off or bounded by their contours, which appear the same whether they fall on one particular set of cells on the retina or on another: as you shift your gaze even slightly to one side of the number at the bottom of the page, a totally new set of cones is stimulated, yet the shape you see remains the same. In the world of hearing—not JND's of pitch or loudness, but coherent sounds and melodies: simply raising the key in which you play or whistle a melody alters every single note, yet the tune itself remains the same (and in fact the change of key may go unrecognized). In both cases, the form we perceive remains constant, though the points of color or the musical notes may be completely changed.

Before we undertake detailed psychophysical measurement, before we seek to understand the underlying physiological mechanisms,* we must discover the rules that govern the appearance of shapes and forms.

Contours, Shapes, and Figures.   Let us start with the fact that although any contour divides the stimulation at the eye into two regions, the shape of both regions cannot be simultaneously observed: only one shape or the other will be seen at any one moment in time, although they may well alternate under prolonged viewing. The side whose shape is visible is called the *figure:* it usually seems to be interposed between the observer and the *ground,* which seems to extend some indeterminate distance behind the figure. Look at Figure 5-8A: as we noted in the previous chapter, either a black vase or two white

---

* Several Gestaltist attempts were made to deduce the true nature of the nervous system by speculating about the kinds of physiological processes that might account for the ways in which perception is organized. Instead of individual specific nerve energies, for example, Gestaltists tended to look for more massive brain processes (analogous to forms, rather than to point-sensations), such as direct current electrical flows from one region to another. These unorthodox speculations seem unnecessary today, however, in view of the tremendously complex picture of the workings of the brain which we have seen evolving in the last chapter (pp. 64–67).

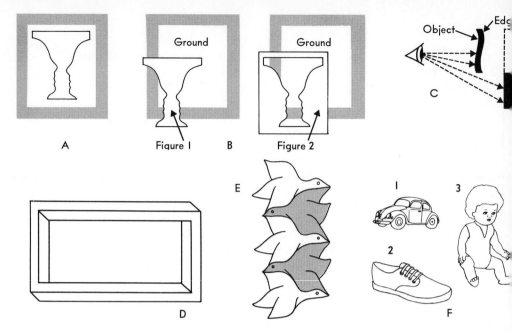

Figure 5-8. **The one-sidedness of outline contours and of objects' edges.** *At (A), either a vase (B) or two faces (B) can be seen as figure. At (B), each alternative is illustrated in terms of the physical arrangement that would correspond to it. This one-sidedness of a contour—which delineates a shape to only one of the two areas it separates—is characteristic of real objects' edges as well. At (C), note that as your gaze crosses the edge of the nearer surface, there is an abrupt increase in distance to the next surface, which normally extends behind the nearer one, out of sight. Figural contours do not share all the characteristics of objects' edges, however, since the former can shift the direction in which they are one-sided as you look from one region of the same contour to another, while real objects' edges cannot do so. To illustrate this difference, trace the lines around the "impossible object" at (D) (after Penrose and Penrose; Hochberg), or try to see the heads of both a white and a dark bird at (E) (after Escher).*

faces can be seen; when the vase has the appearance of 1 in Figure 5-8B, it is being perceived as figure.

As we saw (on pp. 58ff), these phenomena were very difficult to explain in terms of a structuralist analysis into point-sensations, and the Gestaltists offered them in evidence for that reason. We should note, however, that the contour of a figure behaves in some ways like the edge of an object, which by its very nature has a shape on only one side, since past that edge the object's surface ceases to exist (see Figure 5-8C). Is the fact that figural contours have shape in only one direction the result of our past experiences with the edges of objects? This is not known at present. We do know, however, that it is not simply a matter of thinking about figures as though they were objects, since a figure can be inconsistent in ways that objects cannot (Figure 5-8D and E).*

* The fact that we can talk meaningfully about the parts and subregions of a figure, as in Figure 5-8D and E, demonstrates that although the point-sensations of the structuralist were too small to serve as adequate units of analysis, the entire figure, as sometimes proposed by *Gestalt* theory, is too large for the purpose, and that the really appropriate unit for the analysis of form has yet to be found.

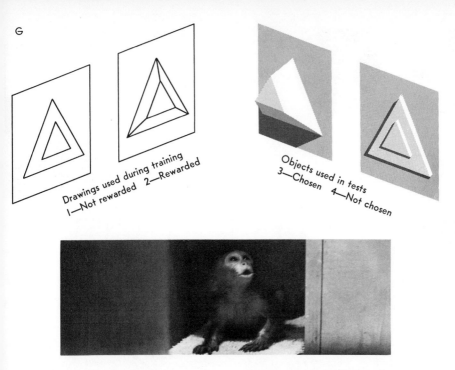

Drawings used during training
1—Not rewarded 2—Rewarded

Objects used in tests
3—Chosen 4—Not chosen

Do we recognize outlined shapes because we have learned to associate line draw-ings with objects' edges much as we learn a foreign language at school? Are out-lines drawn on paper merely learned symbols for the edges of things in the world? No. A child who had been raised without ever having had any opportunity to associate pictures with either objects or with object names (and who had seen very few pictures at all), still could correctly identify the pictured objects shown in (F) (Hochberg and Brooks). Monkeys who had been rewarded for choosing the line drawing of the tridimensional object (G2) chose the real tridimensional object (G3) as against the alternative shown at (G4) (Zimmermann and Hochberg).

Moreover, this phenomenon is not simply the result of our having learned to associate drawings with objects, that is, of learning that outlines "stand for" objects' edges: A child does not have to learn specifically to see outline drawings by associating pictures with objects (Figure 5-8F)—as one might learn a foreign language—and neither do infant monkeys (Figure 5-8G), so that there is no present reason to consider that the properties that contours share with objects' edges are the result of learning.

Ambiguous Stimuli and the Laws of Organization.   Since a contour can produce a shape in either of two directions, it is ambiguous. How can we tell in advance, which shape will be perceived?

The patterns shown in Figure 5-9 are all ambiguous. Changing the patterns in various ways, changes the ease with which each of the alternative arrange-ments of shapes is seen. In this manner, these stimuli lend themselves to a systematic study of the conditions which cause one form rather than another to be perceived.

A number of "laws" of organization have emerged from the study of such ambiguous stimuli (although they shouldn't really be called "laws" at this stage in their exploration).

Higher-Order
Variables
in Perception

85

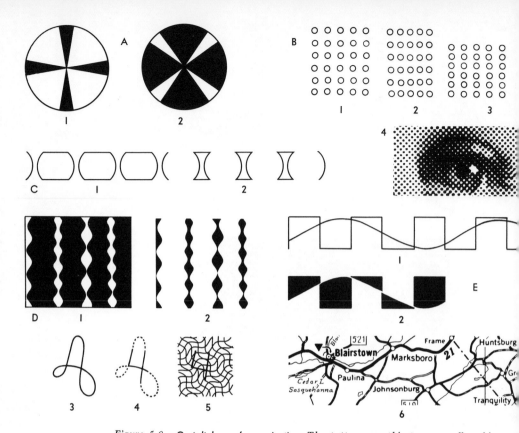

Figure 5-9. **Gestalt laws of organization.** *The patterns on this page are all ambiguous. That is, you can easily see more than one shape in each of them. By making some change in a pattern and observing how that change affects the relative ease of seeing each of the alternative shapes, Max Wertheimer, followed by other Gestalt psychologists (notably Koffka and W. Köhler), compiled a long list of factors that influence the perception of shape. Five of their most important "laws of organization" are illustrated here. (A)* **Area.** *The smaller a closed region, the more it tends to be seen as figure. Thus, as the area of the white cross decreases from 1 to 2, its tendency to be seen as figure increases. (B)* **Proximity.** *Dots or objects that are close together tend to be grouped together. In (1), you can see either horizontal rows or vertical columns with equal ease. As the dots get closer together horizontally, as in (2), horizontal rows emerge as figure; with increased vertical proximity (3), vertical columns appear. Examine the enlarged print of the eye at (4). How does this law contribute to TV or to photoreproductions? (C)* **Closedness.** *Areas with closed contours tend to be seen as figure more than do those with open contours. At (1), profiles of TV screens appear, at (2), profiles of applecores, in accordance with this principle. These three laws are easy enough to measure and test; there are other laws however, of equal or greater importance, that can readily be demonstrated in an intuitive or common-sense manner, but which are extremely difficult to define in an objective, measurable fashion. Two of these challenging factors are shown in (D) and (E). (D)* **Symmetry.** *The more symmetrical a closed region, the more it tends to be seen as figure. Do you see white columns on a black ground in (1), or black columns on a white ground? Which do you see in (2)? (E)* **Good continuation.** *That arrangement of figure and ground tends to be seen which will make the fewest changes or interruptions in straight or smoothly-curving lines or contours. This is one of the most important of the laws of organization. The pattern at (1), for example, is almost always seen as a smooth sine wave superimposed on a square wave. This is in opposition to the law of closedness, which would cause the perception of something like (2). Can you now explain why the number 4 is more effectively concealed at (3) than at (5), even though there are more extraneous lines to confuse you at (5)? How does this law contribute to the reading the map at (6)?*

Some of these laws, such as those of *area, proximity,* and *closedness* (Figure 5-9A, B, and C) are amenable to measurement, and to quantitative statement. Can the other laws of organization, such as *symmetry* and *good continuation* (Figure 5-9D and E), also be treated quantitatively and objectively?

Simplicity and the Minimum Principle
as Laws of Combination

If we examine Figure 5-9 D and E, a pattern emerges. What we observe seems to be the simplest of the possible arrangements. A more obvious example of this principle appears in Figure 5-10. Both patterns are equally good views of the same cube. Why does 1 appear in 3D while 2 does not? Because 1 is *simpler* in 3D and 2 is *simpler* as a flat pattern. A pattern thus seems to appear flat if it is *simpler* (in some sense we still have to define) to see it that way; conversely, it appears to be tridimensional if it is simpler in three dimensions than it is in two. The principle appears to be this: that our nervous systems organize the perceived world in whatever way will keep changes and differences to a *minimum*.

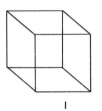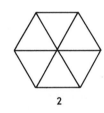

I   2

Figure 5-10. Tridimensionality as a function of organizational simplicity. Patterns (1) and (2) are equally accurate drawings of a wire cube, yet one is easy to see as a tridimensional cube (1), while the other remains a flat pattern (2). Why this difference? In order to see (1) as a flat pattern, or to see (2) as a tridimensional one, you have to break the good continuation of the lines, to make the figure less simple; that is, you see one as tridimensional, the other as flat, depending on which way a simpler *organization is achieved (Kopfermann). This is a powerful principle, if we can find some objective way of measuring simplicity.*

Let us now return to Leonardo da Vinci's depth cues, with which we started the whole problem of combining perceptual parts into the objects and events of the perceived world (pp. 34ff). How do these depth cues fit this law of simplicity, this minimum principle?

In Figure 5-11A, each of the cues (with the exception of familiar size, which is not a very effective cue, anyway, p. 78) appears to be explainable as a special case of the minimum principle in operation. In response to the relative size cue at 1, isn't it simpler to see three equal rectangles at different distances (1″) than three unequal ones at the same distance (1′)? In response to the linear perspective cue at 2, to see an equal-sided square flat in the plane of the ground (2″) rather than an upright trapezoid (2′)? In response to the interposition cue at 3, to see two squares, one before the other (3″), rather than an inverted L and a rectangle in the same plane (3′)? If we were willing to accept the minimum principle as being innate (or acquired very soon after birth *), then at least some of the

---

* Remember that, at present, there is very little difference to the perception psychologist between "innate" and "learned-in-very-early-infancy." See p. 71.

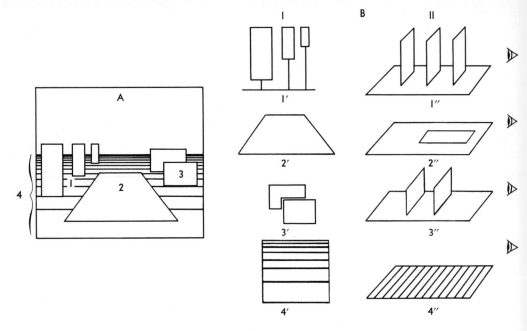

Figure 5-11. The depth cues as cases of organizational simplicity. (A) A simple picture using four monocular depth cues: (1) relative size; (2) linear perspective; (3) interposition; and (4) texture-density gradient. (B) Compare each cue as a flat pattern in an upright plane (column I) and as the tridimensional arrangement it represents (column II). Which seems simpler in each case, the arrangement in (I) or (II)? If organizational simplicity were an innate operating characteristic of the nervous system, what would this figure imply about depth perception?

monocular depth cues may be innate as well, because they are simple consequences of the minimum principle.

This law of simplicity looks like a very powerful principle—if we can be sure that it really is a principle at all! The trouble with it is this: How can we know what is simpler until *after* we have seen which way an ambiguous picture appears? How can we know this in advance of looking at it?

The Psychophysics of Form and Motion

Can we decide, objectively, what shape is the simplest of any set of alternatives? This is one of the most far-reaching challenges we face in the study of perception today. How can we measure simplicity? See Figure 5-12A: If we can find such a measure, we may be able to find the higher-order variables with which to predict shape and form perception, and put the Gestaltists' insights to work. If we cannot, we will have only our intuitions to rely upon in this task—and in the many other tasks in which organization is important.

Information and Redundancy in the Psychophysics of Static Shape. In Figure 5-12A, several shapes are arranged in an order of their increasing apparent complexity as two-dimensional patterns. What *physical* variable increases from one shape to the next?

Suppose you had to tell someone how to construct each pattern. In each case, the amount of information you would have to give him would increase. How can we measure this information? There are many kinds of physical measurement we can make, which will be different from one shape to the next and which would seem to be related to simplicity of organization. The problem remains this, however: to discover *which* measure, out of all the possible measures of shape complexity, predicts which of the alternative shapes will in fact be perceived.

In order to answer this question, we need a special set of tools. We have to find some kind of stimulus pattern that produces two clearly different alternative perceptual organizations, and that will permit the complexity of one of the alternatives to be systematically varied, while the complexity of the other alternative is kept constant. In this way, we will be able to study the psychophysical relationship between some measure of the complexity of each alternative form, on the one hand, and the strength of the tendency to see that form, on the other. The kinds of reversible-perspective pictures shown in Figure 5-12A provide us with just such material for studying the psychophysics of form, since the flat, two-dimensional shape varies from one figure to the next, while the solid three-dimensional form remains the same for each member in the series. Thus, each pattern in Figure 5-12A can be described either as an arrangement of flat shapes or as a three-dimensional object. The simpler any 2D arrangement, the more we should tend to see that picture in 2D; conversely, the more complex the 2D arrangement, the more we tend to see it as 3D (since the 3D form must be the same and, therefore, of identical simplicity, for all views of any object). As the *number of angles,* the *number of continuous lines*, and the *average number of different angles* increase in each pattern, the tendency to see the flat arrangement decreases and the apparent tridimensionality of the form increases,* although there are almost certainly other factors as well that we have not yet found.

We seem to have made a first step toward discovering and using objective measures of the minimum principle, and toward bringing the *Gestalt* laws into quantitative and measurable form. A psychophysics of shape and form now seems to be as possible to achieve as does one of lightness and color.

The problem of organization is much larger than that of predicting the appearance of ambiguous pictured shapes and forms, however. Discovering ways of measuring simplicity of *organization* becomes even more challenging when we extend our interests to include the perception of motion and of forms other than those of drawn or printed pictures.

The Psychophysics of Form in Motion.   If the concealed bird in Figure 1-2C once moves, it snaps into visibility. The views of Figure 5-13 come to life, and move compellingly into the third dimension as they follow each other in

---

* The measure of 2D complexity used in Figure 5-12B is obtained as follows: $C_i = [a + d + 2(c)]$, where $C_i =$ the relative 2D complexity of each pattern in a family of patterns; $a =$ the number of angles within that pattern, $d =$ the average number of different angles, and $c =$ the number of continuous lines. Each of these variables is scored on a 0–10 scale, in which the value of 10 means that the particular pattern being scored has the highest number, on the variable in question, of all the members of the family to which it belongs.

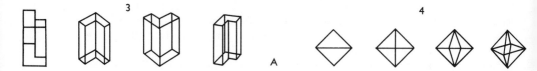

Figure 5-12. Measuring simplicity: information and organization. So far, we have relied on intuition in order to decide which of two organizations is simpler. The objective and quantitative measurement of organizational simplicity poses one of the most challenging problems in the study of perception today, since it seems to be the key to a great variety of other problems. Its study, however, is just beginning. (A) The different views of each object in (1) through (4) are arranged in order of increasing tridimensionality in each row. According to the hypothesis of Figure 5-10, this means that the two-dimensional alternatives must be getting less simple and more complex as we read from left to right in each row. What measurable physical characteristics of the patterns in (1) through (4) increase as we move from left to right in each row?

(B) The number of interior angles, the average number of different angles, and the number of continuous lines, can be combined to provide a fair measure of complexity. In the graph, the horizontal axis shows the complexity measures for each of the 2D (two-dimensional) patterns in (A); the vertical axis shows the apparent tridimensionality of the same patterns, as they were judged by scores of observers (Hochberg and Brooks).

(C) Two closely related measures of figural simplicity have recently been proposed and used by Fred Attneave: One method requires subjects to guess whether each successive square in a sheet of graph paper is black, white, or brown. They are given no advance information about what the correct pattern (1) looks like, only whether they are right or wrong on each guess. Subjects made only 13 to 26 errors for the entire sheet of 4,000 squares—immensely less than they would have made had they been guessing at random on each square. Where did their knowledge come from?

Having discovered one part of the figure, a subject could then make some pretty good guesses about the remainder, since areas are compact, lines and slopes

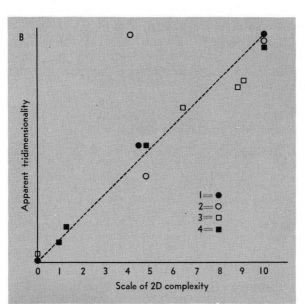

are regular, and the shape is symmetrical: that is, (1) is a "good" or simple figure. Thus, one measure of simplicity is the predictability of the whole from the part—that is, the degree to which, by knowing some of the parts of the figure, a subject can correctly guess the rest of the parts. Some parts of any shape are usually highly predictable, like the continuation of a straight line; these are called redundant, or uninformative. Other parts are not predictable, and it is these unpredictable segments that provide the information that is needed if the shape

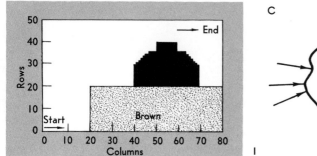

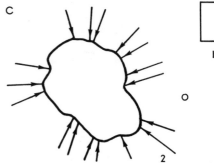

is to be identified or reproduced. In (2) is one of a number of outline shapes that subjects were asked to reproduce as closely as possible, using only 10 dots to represent each shape. The small arrows point to the places at which subjects most frequently choose to place the dots: the strategic bends and curves where the contour is most different from a simple, straight predictable line.

Other things equal, the fewer the bends or angles (and the fewer the lines), the simpler and the more predictable the shape. This kind of measure of simplicity was designed for problems of shape-identification or communication, so that it seems to be a little removed from the problem of figural organization as such. However, we have seen in B that a very closely related measure of simplicity did appear when we attempted to predict the relative frequency-of-appearance of alternative figural organizations.

time. The door swings open in A; in B, if we alternate patterns X and Y in rapid succession, apparent motion occurs in the direction shown by the arrow, flipping through the third dimension.

Figure 5-13. **Shape and motion.** *(A1) Five different shapes, or a door of constant shape swinging through the third dimension? When these patterns are viewed successively, as in a motion picture, the constant shape of the door and its path through space are equally and overwhelmingly compelling. Flip the right-hand pages, from here to p. 99, as shown in (2), looking at the marginal figure (I). (B) If X alternates with Y, we could see two different shapes in different places at successive intervals in time, or we could see a single constant triangle, turning over through the third dimension, as shown by the solid path (1); this latter alternative predominates.*

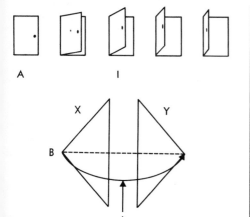

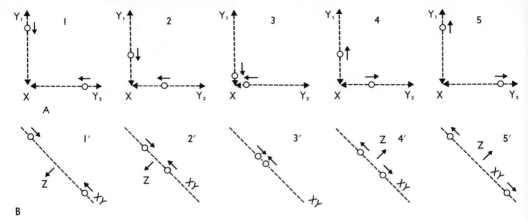

Figure 5-14. The perception of alternative motion organizations. (A) Two lights move at right angles to each other, repeatedly coming together at point (X), then retreating from that point along paths (Y₁), (Y₂). Flip the pages of the book from p. 91 to p. 99, looking at marginal figure (II). We do not see this motion, which is in reality what falls on the retina of our eye, any more than we saw absolute light-intensity or visual angle (Figures 5-1 and 5-5). Instead, the following set of motions are perceived predominantly: (B) The lights appear to approach and retreat from each other along the diagonal (XY); the diagonal path itself moves up and down along the direction (Z), although this is not very noticeable (Johansson). Flip the pages of the book to visualize the resultant motion. The simplest relative motion is what we see.

We saw in Figure 5-12B that whether a stimulus-pattern will appear flat or solid depends on the relative simplicity of the alternative organizations. Don't these *motions* follow the same principle? In some sense, isn't it simpler to see a single unchanging triangle rotate from X to Y in space, in Figure 5-13B, than to see two different triangles at two different positions? Once again, we can neither accept this intuition nor reject it until we have some way of measuring simplicity.

Suppose that two lights in a dark room move as shown in Figure 5-14A, coming to a point of contact (X), and then moving away again along paths Y₁, Y₂. What will we see? *Not* the motion just described; instead, corresponding to each of the positions of the lights as shown in 1 through 5, the lights appear to move toward and away from each other on a diagonal line (XY), as shown in B1′ through 5′, and the whole line will move up and down in the direction shown by the arrow (Z). The physical movement which is really present has disappeared and, instead, we see a new set of motions. Is there anything in the stimulation that will explain these new motions, XY and Z? There is. If we analyze the real movement into a set of component vectors by first extracting the motion which the two lights follow with respect to each other, and then represent the remaining motion as a separate vector, what we will have is precisely what is shown by XY and Z in Figure 5-14B.

Analyzing a number of different experiments of this sort suggests the following rule: First, we see a static background; next, with this as a frame of reference, we see whatever motion (vector Z) is common to all the moving parts; lastly and most prominently, against this common motion, we see whatever component motions remain left over, furnishing the relative motions of the parts.*

Thus, *just that arrangement of motions is perceived which entails the least number of changes*. Not all changes are to be weighed equally, however, in attempting to apply this principle. Certain kinds of change are more to be avoided than others, and this is important in an attempt to define what is meant by simplicity. Our perceptions of objects remain as constant and as rigid as possible. In Figure 5-13 we perceive whatever motions are necessary to allow the door to remain a rectangle, or to allow the triangle to retain the lengths and positions of its sides unchanged.

The monocular, stationary view of any object is ambiguous, as we have seen in Figure 4-4. Many distal stimulus-objects can produce the same image at the eye. On the other hand, with each successive view of a rotating object, new information has been presented to our perceptual system. How many different rigid, constant objects could produce at the eye the same sequence as those in Figure 5-15A1 and 2?

* The shortest movement of any part therefore determines what common motion will be seen. If two movements are the same in other respects, the one with the shorter path (or the lower velocity) determines the common motion, forming the moving framework within which the remaining motions occur; if two or more component motions are equal in magnitude and direction, they will appear as a single motion.

Figure 5-15. Organizational simplicity and the kinetic depth effect. (A) Each view of the cube at (1) is ambiguous, in that each can be seen as either a flat pattern or as a tridimensional cube. Each of the triangles at (2) is, individually, different but quite flat-appearing. However, if these are the successive views of a rotating object, one could still see a succession of changing flat patterns, but it is much simpler to see a single rotating tridimensional object, of constant shape, and this is what one sees (Wallach and O'Connell). Flip the pages from p. 91 to p. 99, looking at marginal figures (III) and (IV). (B) If views (1) through (5) were presented in succession, you could see a set of roughly rectangular patterns, in each of 5 arrangements (marginal figure V) (Gibson). What is the simpler alternative?

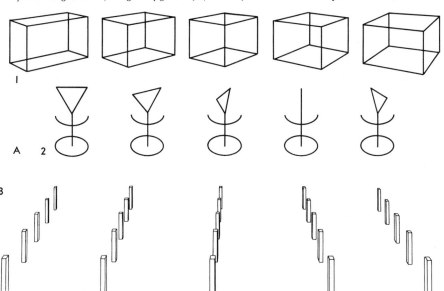

In consequence, objects whose spatial forms are ambiguous when they are viewed while they are stationary usually spring into three dimensions when they are rotated. This is called *kinetic depth effect*.* Even with the rotation, though, some ambiguity remains. At least theoretically, instead of a cube rotating in Figure 5-15, one might be confronted by a highly improbable set of sticks which grow and shrink and change their relative positions—or by a movie of a rotating cube, which is itself a set of flat pictures. However, motions in the optic array are usually caused not only by the movement of objects, but also by the movements of the observer as well. How does this change matters?

TOWARD A PSYCHOPHYSICS OF SPACE-PERCEPTION: DETERMINING THE PERCEPTION OF THE REAL WORLD FOR A MOVING OBSERVER

When the study of perception started with pure sensations and attempted to build up from these to an understanding of our perceptions of the physical world, there seemed to be no way to gain unambiguous information about the world of objects, space, and motion by means of our eyes alone. We shall now see that, if we consider the higher-order variables which result from the observer's own motions, the stimulation at the eye is completely unambiguous—at least in principle.

Berkeley "Refuted"

A single view of a single object may be ambiguous, but successive presentations reduce this ambiguity. Similarly, as we start to assemble a number of different objects into a single static scene, one spatial arrangement becomes more economical than any of the alternatives. In Figure 4-3B, the relative size difference between boys 1 and 2, the convergence of the lines, the interposition of cards 4 and 5, the texture-density gradient—all of these are *individually* simpler if the scene is perceived as a whole, for, *collectively* the economies of each reinforce the others.

If we now add the effects of the motion of the observer himself, the informational economy of seeing only one spatial arrangement—the true or veridical arrangement—becomes overwhelmingly greater than that of any other. In fact, it appears that, if he uses all of the visual information that is available, *there is no way at all of fooling an observer, once we let him determine his own movements*.

Imagine a row of fenceposts viewed from one end, as in Figure 5-15B. As you walk past it to the right, you will get successive views 2 and 1; as you walk past it to the left, you will get successive views 4 and 5. A succession of such views could give you visual information about *where you are looking*

---

* Moreover, once having been endowed with spatial form by the kinetic depth effect, a pattern that previously had appeared to be flat will subsequently appear solid (this may be important to any theory of perceptual learning). (H. Wallach and D. N. O'Connell. The kinetic depth effect. *J. exp. Psychol.,* 1948, 38, 310–324.)

from within the scene, and how you are moving around in it—as long as you assume that the objects are fixed and rigid.

Now add to this the fact that *you can change your view at your own volition.* As long as you were forced to sit passively, there is no way, in principle, that you could distinguish between the succession of scenes shown in Figure 5-15, which might be the successive frames of a movie film, and the change in viewpoint (called *motion parallax*) which would result from real motion in a real, three-dimensional world. If, on the other hand, you are free to walk left and right, or to move your head around, there will be changes in the optic array which are precisely tied to your voluntary movements, in the case of a real fence in real space, but which would not occur in the case of the movie. If you are free to initiate this visual *feedback* (the change in the optic array which results from motions which were made by the observer himself), then it becomes difficult or impossible to fool you about the world.

Does this imply some sort of unconscious inference (pp. 56ff.), some sort of figuring out what the true state of affairs is? Not necessarily. There are higher-order stimulus-variables in the normal world of the moving observer to which these perceptions may correspond.

Figure 5-16. **The optical expansion pattern received by a moving observer.** (*A*) *Hold the book at about arm's length with one hand, and hold your little finger of the other hand so that its width just fits between points (X-X') at (1), and as illustrated at (2). Next, bring the book toward your eyes, as smoothly and uniformly as possible. What happens to the visual angle subtended by the distance between points (X) and (X')? Repeat this procedure, but this time pay attention to the relative change in distance between (Y-X) as compared to (X-X'): The distance between points in the optic array expands as you approach the surface which contains those points. (B) The pattern with which the distances between points expand and the rate at which the expansions occur offer information about the observer's distance from the surface, how fast he is approaching or receding from it, at what angle he is traveling with respect to it, and where he will collide with the surface if he continues to approach it. The "flow pattern" created by the points in a surface which is being approached along a 45° path is shown here; the directions and lengths of arrows point the direction and rate of expansion, respectively, of each point in the optic array (after Gibson et al.).*

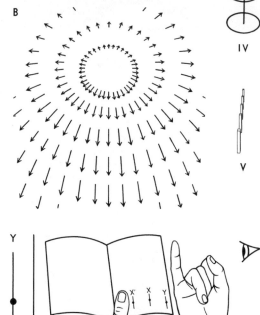

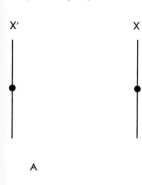

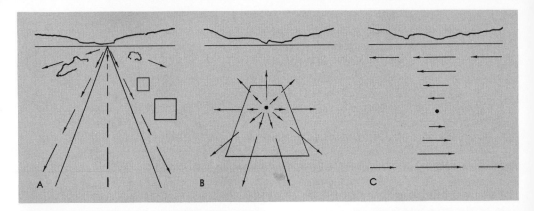

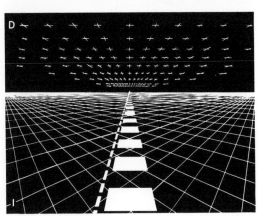

Figure 5-17. **Flow patterns for different elementary movements of the observer.** *At (A), the optical expansion pattern your eye receives when walking, driving, or flying toward the horizon (straight ahead); at (B), what confronts a pilot who is heading for a touchdown at the point; at (C), the view you receive as you look, at right angles to your movement, at the point shown (out of the side windows of a car, for example). In any case, the point at which you would hit the surface is the single stationary point in the expansion pattern. Such elementary flow patterns may provide components with which to analyze the optical movements and positions in space (A, B, C after Gibson). At (D), we see the "contact analog" (1) now being developed, by General Electric, to present to the operators of high-speed vehicles readily grasped information about the vehicles' movements, by means of such flow patterns and texture-density gradients. The contact analog is a computer-operated television-type tube which presents to the pilot a pictorial display that is visually analogous to contact flight, giving to instrument flight the freedom of visual flight conditions. The visual cues displayed on the vertical screen form the three-dimensioned background and a ribbon-like pathway along which the airplane is flown. Deviations from the intended course or altitude cause the airplane to appear displaced from the pathway accordingly. Contrast this single display with the confusing aggregate of instruments a pilot now must use (2).*

Every time an observer moves toward any rigid surface, the elements in the field undergo a process of expansion, and this *gradient of expansion* forms a pattern which will be different for each orientation of surface, for each direction and speed of motion of the observer, and for each distance of the observer from that surface (see Figures 5-16 and 5-17).

I

We do not yet know how well we can actually use these rich sources of purely visual potential-information about the world (see pp. 80, 81). The importance of self-initiated visual feedback cues is strongly supported by the fact that the kitten who was confined in the cart shown in Figure 4-13, p. 48, failed to "learn to see" as adequately as its moving partner, even though they both received equally varied visual experience, but this does not mean that we take full advantage of these higher-order variables. Perform this simple experiment yourself. Choose a long, straight street or highway, and walk with a steady pace along it while you make the following judgment: Do the sides of the street converge toward the horizon, or do they appear to stretch away from you in completely parallel arrangement? If they appear to converge at all, what does this imply about your use of the available information?

o

o

II

When we took up the problems of space perception in Chapter 3, we started with the puzzle of explaining how we see the world so correctly, with so little information on which to base our perceptions. The problem has now been reversed. Considering how much stimulus information there appears to be potentially available to an observer, we must wonder why his perceptions of space are not always perfectly correct.

III

The Limited Uses of a Psychophysics of Space

We have learned a great deal about the higher-order variables of shape, form, and space in recent years, and we have learned much more about what kinds of variables we should look to next, and how to study them. What we have to look for in the way of perceptual learning has undergone a major revision, a start has been made toward understanding and measuring the phenomena of organization, and we can approach constancies and illusions in a new and hopeful manner.

IV

This very promise of success, however, should not blind us to the fact that this is a much narrower achievement than it appeared to be when the structuralists first set it up as a goal. Initially, the purpose of studying sensations was to enable us to explain and predict our observations of *all* the world and its contents—including such nonphysical variables and events as *anger* and *quarrels, smiles* and *affection,* that is, the relationships between people which are important to us as individuals, and as psychologists. It seemed to be guaranteed that if we could discover the sensations and their laws of combination, we should be able eventually to explain the perception of a smile as readily as the perception of an apple. But the idea of sensations as elementary variables is gone, and with it the possibility of using the sensations to explain or predict anything at all. It is true that we do have some new sets of elements which may prove useful—the edges and combining laws of shape perception are of some use in the study of pictorial and symbolic communication (pp. 83–90), and some of the qualities of surfaces (p. 80) may be important in understanding how we perceive facial expressions (which are,

V

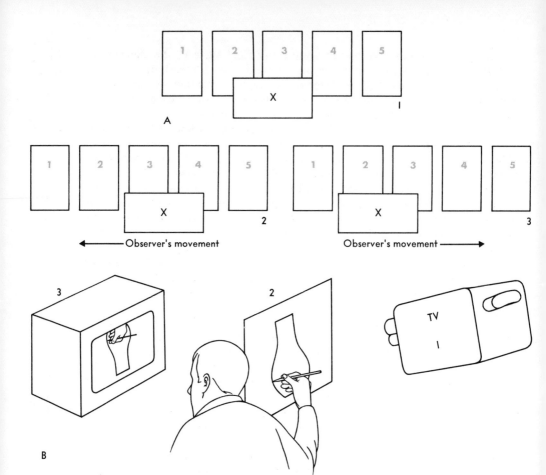

Figure 5-18. How voluntary movement and visual feedback make spatial arrangements completely unambiguous—in theory, but not in fact. *(A) When you move, and change the optic array from (1) to (2), you receive visual feedback from your movements which make the visual information completely unambiguous. If you suddenly decide to move in the opposite direction, from the starting position shown at (1), the proximal stimulus will change from (1) to (3). What other conceivable distal stimulus arrangement could produce these specific visual changes, so precisely correlated with your own movements? Theoretically, then, there is ample information in the optic array to enable us to make perfectly accurate judgments about space—if we could in fact use all of that information—and no illusions should be possible in real life with a free observer, nor should constancy ratios ever be anything but 1.00 (see p. 52). (B) The actual use to which we can put our visual feedback has been subjected to experimental test only in recent years, using TV cameras (1) to view the distal stimulus situation (2), while the observer sees the results of his actions by viewing what the TV camera transmits to the monitor (3). This arrangement permits the experimenter to interfere with the feedback by inverting, reversing, displacing, or even delaying the picture presented on the monitor (K. U. and W. Smith).*

after all, changes in the spatial arrangement of the skin of the face). Even so, we must not expect that our social perceptions are built up out of perceived surfaces, any more than surfaces are out of sensations of points.

In the next chapter, we shall turn our attention to what little we do know about social perception and communication.

I

SUMMARY

A higher-order variable is a measured relationship between individual measures. In this chapter, we considered how the use of higher-order variables of stimulation might solve many of the problems of sensory analysis that arose in the previous chapter—particularly, problems of color- and size-constancy and of the organization of form and motion. For example, ratios of the light-energy of adjacent regions in the optic array will predict the colors we see (and explain the phenomena of constancy and of contrast) far better than will measures of each region considered separately.

Another simple higher-order variable is a *gradient,* which is the rate at which some measured property changes uniformly from one end of some region to the other. Surfaces at some slant to the line-of-sight produce characteristic gradients of texture-density in the optic array, providing a higher-order variable of stimulation that automatically takes distance into account and, thereby, providing a possible explanation of size-constancy in particular and distance-perception in general.

The organization of form remains a somewhat more difficult problem. *Gestalt* theorists used ambiguous patterns (which lend themselves to the study of what causes one form or motion rather than another to be perceived) to derive numerous "laws" of organization. Most of these can be summarized under the "law" of simplicity ("we see what is simplest to see")— a law whose application obviously depends on our being able to measure simplicity. Since in recent years first steps have been made toward the objective measurement of simplicity, predictive laws of shape perception and of motion perception seem as possible to achieve as do those of color and size perception.

Whether by early perceptual learning or by inborn arrangement, our nervous systems seem to choose those ways of seeing the world that keep perceived surfaces and objects as simple and constant as possible, and this fact offers a very different picture of space perception than that of Chapter 4: Earlier, the eyes seemed to provide only ambiguous information about the world of space and motion; now, when we consider the higher-order variables produced in the optic array by the observer's own movements the available visual stimulation is potentially quite unambiguous.

This promise—that higher-order variables of stimulation will explain our perceptions of physical space as simply as other variables predict our perceptions of colors—should not suggest, however, that surfaces are the elements for building all perception (including, for example, the perception of social qualities and events).

O

II

III

IV

V

Social Perception and Communication

The unifying aim of all the questions considered in the previous chapters was to discover how we perceive (and how we portray) the world of physical objects and events. Such problems are still important, but they can no longer be considered to be fundamental to all other perceptual questions. It is easier, of course, to experiment with points and lines and colors than with, say, facial expressions, and it is easier to describe what we have done in such experiments because we have excellent standardized measuring instruments for size and color and almost none at all for expression; but this fact does not imply that we must

6

understand the perception of points, colors, and surfaces before we shall be ready to understand the perception of facial expressions.

One recurring objection to the study of most of the phenomena of social perception is that they are so clearly the result of learning. The same argument would have to be made about the perception of physical objects and events, however. In Berkeley's original discussion of space perception, he maintained that "As we see distance so we see magnitude. And we see both in the same way that we see shame or anger in the looks of a man. . . . Without . . . experience we should no more have taken blushing for a sign of shame than of gladness." This proposition was widely accepted, but since it did not prevent the active investigation of both distance and magnitude, neither should it prevent the study of the perception of shame or anger. Though their effectiveness may be the result of learning, the stimuli of social perception are themselves the tools by which much of the prediction and control of human behavior—including learning—is achieved in practice. The great problems of human motivation are implicated in this area, and it is all the more exciting that we have so little information here. The centuries of preoccupation with the perception of the physical world has left this an open area for adventure and exploration.

The main problem in this chapter is one of *direction*. As long as we could study the perception of physical events in hopes of finding the fundamental elements and laws by which to explain our perceptions of other and perhaps more interesting events, the goals and the promise were clear. We no longer have that rainbow ahead of us, and the problem of what we should study becomes somewhat more serious, considering the immense number of kinds of perception, none more "fundamental" than the others, which we might take up. At least initially, therefore, we should try to keep in mind the promise of each field of research in social perception—the promise of where it might lead, and of what uses it might serve.

SOCIAL EFFECTS ON PSYCHOPHYSICAL MEASURES

In discussing sensory psychophysics (p. 9), we noted that the observer's expectations, interests, and motivation might affect the measurement of thresholds. Social psychologists first turned to using these "errors" for their own purposes about 30 years ago. This was followed by a tremendous surge of interest during the post-World War II drive to bring psychology out of the laboratory and into the area of improving human society. The available perceptual laboratory methods were those that had been devised to study color and space, so that the study of social perception started with these methods.

Attempts to bring social relevance to these psychophysical measures may be grouped under two headings: socially produced distortions of psychophysical correspondence, and socially altered recognition thresholds.

Distortions of Psychophysical Correspondence

We include as *social variables* all the effects of past experience, interest, reward, punishment, expectation, and so forth, which we would expect to be different for observers who come from different social classes or backgrounds. Examples are familiarity with coins of different denomination, or with words of varying vulgarity. Social variables have been shown to affect subjects' judgments of the magnitude of such physical dimensions as size, length, color, and position (Figure 6-1A). Many of these effects, however, are very small; * indeed, after more than a decade of quite intensive research in this area, it is not yet clear what reliable and reproducible effects exist.

A second way was found to use the available psychophysical apparatus and methods for social-psychological research. This approach is still popular today, and it deserves separate consideration.

Recognition Thresholds of Social Stimuli

If we weaken or *impoverish* the seeing conditions, as we might by making a slide projection too dim, too brief or too out of focus, we can then gradually improve the visibility and find the threshold (in terms of amount of light, duration of the exposure, or degree of misfocus) for recognizing different social stimuli. Thus, in the typical *perceptual defense* experiment (Figure 6-1B3), "bad" stimuli are found to have higher thresholds than do neutral stimuli. That is, they have to be brighter, clearer, or projected longer in order to be correctly reported. What makes these effects particularly interesting is that they seem to support Sigmund Freud's theories about the unconscious determinants of behavior: Don't these words first have to be correctly recognized in order to be seen as a potential threat, only then to be countered by the defense of a raised threshold? Doesn't this in turn imply the existence of *two* observers within each body, one that recognizes the words and then raises barriers against them, and the other—the one with which we are acquainted in ourselves—that sees only what the first unconscious observer permits him to see? This preperceptual observation, or *subception* (which is similar to the doctrine of unconscious inference we discussed in pp. 53–57), achieved recent notoriety when commercial proposals were made to use *subliminal,* or unnoticeable, advertising (Figure 6-1B4). It was assumed that the viewer would be particularly unresistant to unconsciously recognized advertising, because he could not identify the sources and examine the content critically. Less diabolically, it was proposed that emotion-producing words and symbols could be inserted between the successive frames of movies and TV shows to heighten the entertainment value.

Unfortunately both for the theoretical questions concerning the existence of an unconscious observer, and for the dramatic commercial ventures which were to be based on the efficacy of these preperceptual phenomena, the effects are neither large nor well corroborated. The Freudian theory needs more direct manifestation, if the intent is to provide a laboratory demonstration, and the uses of the advertiser will be better served by other aspects of the study of social perception.

Even if these phenomena were large and reliable, however, how would they help us to understand the perception of people and of social events?

---

* In fact, they are usually smaller than the JND of the sensory quality concerned, so that they may well be merely *response biases* (see p. 8).

A

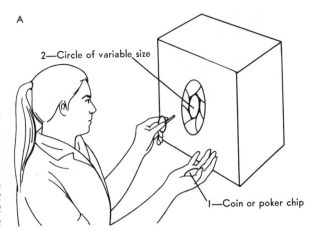

2—Circle of variable size

1—Coin or poker chip

Figure 6-1. Social effects on psychophysical measures. (A) Children from poor families who set a variable circular opening (2) to match the size of a coin (1) overestimated the coin's size more than did rich children (Bruner and Goodman). Similar effects can be obtained by using poker chips instead of coins, and making the chips valuable by experimental procedures in which they can be cashed in for candy; as the chips are rewarded, their estimated size rises (Lambert et al.). The differences between rich and poor children have not proved to be very reliable (Carter and Schooler), though, and in both cases the magnitudes of the effects are small.

(B) Projecting a word or picture out of focus can make it unrecognizable. (1) Improving the focus step by step, pictures of food are recognized earlier by hungry subjects than by sated ones, and so on. This effect is called autism (Murphy et al.; McClelland and Atkinson). Similarly, decreasing the intensity of a projected word or making the reading time too brief makes the word illegible (2). "Dirty" words, or nonsense syllables that had been followed by electric shock, need longer exposure than do neutral words (3). This effect is called perceptual defense, and

seems to imply some kind of unconscious recognition, or subception (McGinnies; Lazarus and McCleary). All these threshold differences are usually quite small and may be due in whole or part to response bias (p. 8), so the extent to which they reflect true differences in perception is still at issue. There is very little chance that subliminal (below-threshold) advertising (4), which has been proposed as an application of these phenomena, will work.

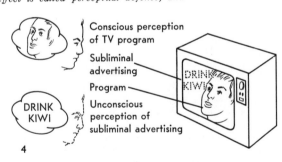

Conscious perception of TV program

Subliminal advertising

Program

Unconscious perception of subliminal advertising

DRINK KIWI

4

B

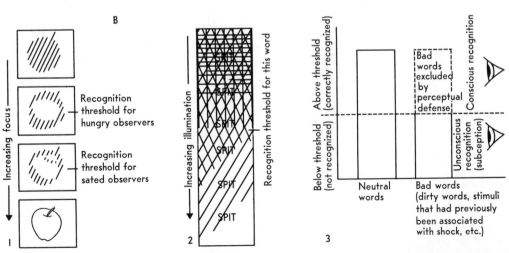

Increasing focus

Recognition threshold for hungry observers

Recognition threshold for sated observers

1

Increasing illumination

Recognition threshold for this word

SPIT

2

Above threshold (correctly recognized)

Below threshold (not recognized)

Neutral words

Bad words excluded by perceptual defense

Bad words (dirty words, stimuli that had previously been associated with shock, etc.)

Conscious recognition

Unconscious recognition (subception)

3

Although real-life situations may be confused, or ambiguous in the sense that different people will perceive the same situation in quite different ways, they are not generally characterized by incredibly poor lighting, by hundredth-of-a-second glimpses, or by an advanced stage of uncorrected myopia. Nevertheless, these are the situations that these experiments in Figure 6-1B emulate. Any generalization from such research to normal social situations must therefore be based on the assumption that one kind of perceptual difficulty is equivalent to all others, and that our perceptual system tackles the problem of deciding, say, whether a new girl is merely coy or genuinely dislikes us, just as it identifies an out-of-focus word.

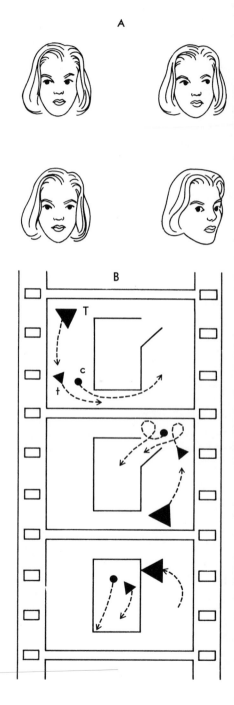

Figure 6-2. Physical properties of social stimuli. (A) Is she looking at me? There is a reciprocal relationship between where the eye must be in its socket, and the direction in which the head is turned, in order that the other person's gaze remains fixed on you. We are remarkably precise in the degree to which we detect that someone is not looking at us; the degree of visual acuity involves detection of differences of about one minute of visual angle, which is about the precision we expect to obtain with such apparently simpler tasks as reading the letters on a chart (p. 25) (Gibson and Pick). (B) Mechanical motion or animate action? In the series of frames from an animated cartoon, the geometrical figures take the complex paths indicated by the dotted lines. Observers trying to report what they see in terms of the mechanical paths of motion would have an immensely complex task. To say, "T chases t and c into the house and closes the door," is far simpler, and this in fact is the kind of action most observers report seeing (Heider and Simmel). In what way is this similar to the operation of the minimum principle in the perception of shape and motion as we discussed these in pp. 87–94?

There is another difficulty in taking such social effects on psychophysical measures as our starting point, however. If the perception of social events were *built up* in some sense out of JND's of color and position, we could apply the results of such threshold experiments as those in Figure 6-1 to social perception; we know from the previous chapters, however, that this is no longer a tenable position. If we could expect the same kinds of distortions of *social* qualities to occur as we find occuring in, say, size (Figure 6-1A), then these findings might become relevant to social perception—but first, we would have to know something about the normal or undistorted qualities of social perception, and this is precisely the field that has been so neglected.

The main reason for such neglect is probably that light and sound are both easy to manipulate and to measure, but the same is simply not true for social events and objects. People and groups are difficult to manipulate experimentally, difficult to measure, and difficult to describe precisely. In recent years, techniques have been found to surmount these difficulties.

THE PERCEPTION OF PEOPLE AND OF OTHER SOCIAL OBJECTS AND EVENTS

Only a few experiments provide a link between the problems of direction, size, motion, and so on studied in the previous chapters, and those involved in the perception of living creatures and of their characteristic properties. The direction of another person's gaze, the size of a social group, the conditions for perceiving living action as opposed to mechanical motion—these kinds of scattered physical questions have been asked about social objects and events (Figure 6-2). Most research has been directed toward quite different kinds of problems, the foremost being how well we can judge other persons' character traits or abilities on the bases of their features or their manner. Although a great deal of the work on the question of how we judge persons and their personalities has been pursued for quite different purposes from that of identifying *what stimuli will produce which experience,* some of the research on this problem is in fact clearly concerned with this problem in social perception, for one or another reason.

Facial Cues to Character Traits and Abilities

There is a long history of unrewarding attempts to identify certain characteristics of facial structure or body types, on the one hand, with honesty vs. dishonesty, stupidity vs. intelligence, amiability vs. hostility, and so on, on the other hand (Figure 6-3A and B). Most people consider themselves good judges of character, and for selecting the candidate for a job the personal interview (or, at least, a photograph pinned to the application blank) remains as testimony to the belief that a person's future actions can be judged by his appearance.

This is a question of perceptual achievement in part (similar in form to the use of depth cues to arrive at a correct perception of space; see pp. 50ff.). How accurately do judges really use facial cues to perceive personal traits, and how do they come to do so? First, of course, we have to be able to measure the traits we are interested in before we can approach this question.

Social Perception and Communication

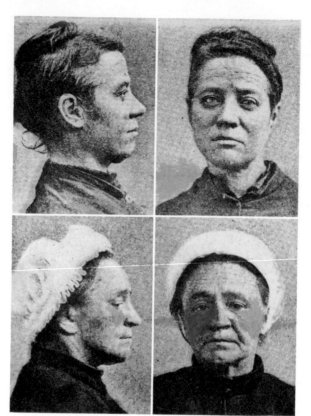

A

Figure 6-3. Physiognomy, physique, and personality. Can personality and character be read in one's face or figure? Common sense suggests it, and many philosophers have thought so for centuries, and reasonably specific schemes have been presented tying face or body to temperament. At (A), two examples of the typical criminal face, according to Lombroso in 1896; at (B), the elementary body types and their traits of character, as described by Sheldon in 1940. Neither of these theories is at all widely accepted today.

B

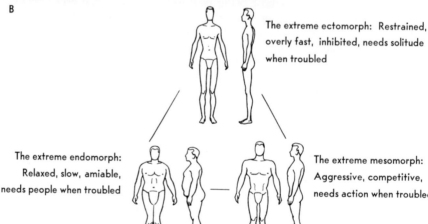

The extreme ectomorph: Restrained, overly fast, inhibited, needs solitude when troubled

The extreme endomorph: Relaxed, slow, amiable, needs people when troubled

The extreme mesomorph: Aggressive, competitive, needs action when troubled

We have reasonably reliable measures for the cluster of abilities represented by the Intelligence Quotient, or IQ. How well is the IQ judged? The experiment summarized in Figure 6-4A tells us two things: that the judges used didn't do very well with the sample of persons used,* and that they did agree with one another (6-4B, C). This second fact implies that the judges are responding consistently and lawfully to something about the social objects, and this, in turn, means that if we can discover what stimulus characteristics they are responding to, we shall be able to predict and control social perception, just as we already can predict much about space and object perception!

In addition to photographs, research in trait perception has used highly simplified drawings (Figure 6-4B), combinations of photographs and character-descriptions, and even shopping lists. In this last case, Mason Haire, a psychologist applying experimental techniques to the problems of market research, presented to two groups of women two identical shopping lists which differed only in that one included instant coffee. The women were to describe the character of the fictitious housewife to whom the list belonged. The instant coffee proved to be a cue to the traits of laziness, lack of thrift, and poor planning, a distressing but useful finding to the makers of instant coffee. This procedure is really over the hazy borderline between the study of perception and the study of attitudes, but the kind of question—that is, what is the effect of varying any given feature?—can be asked by strictly perceptual procedures as well.

How does a cue become a signal for a trait in the first place, and how can it be changed? One popular hypothesis is that by frequently appearing in association with a particular trait, a cue will gain its meaning. This hypothesis is plausible as far as it goes, but it has been insufficiently tested so far, and we face the puzzle of discovering why such associations are formed, since the "physiognomic" theories of personality (Figure 6-3A, B) are not widely accepted any more.

Perhaps what is important is the predominant expression a face suggests, a topic which deserves separate consideration.

Facial Expressions as the Cues to Emotions and Intentions.   The face is an extremely important organ of communication for revealing, concealing, and dissembling states of emotion, desires, feelings, and intentions. We can conceal our social feelings with some effort by maintaining a "poker face"; similarly, we can communicate feelings we do not in fact possess by "acting." Though humans undoubtedly use facial expression to communicate their intentions and their reactions, we know nothing as yet about the natural units—the "words" and "grammar"—of this visual language. Is each facial contortion unique in meaning? Or, as seems much more likely, is there a finite number of kinds of expression, as there is a finite number of words in speech and a finite number of elementary hues out of which all colors can be composed p. 21)? A small number of qualities suffice to account for all the facial

---

*With persons as our stimulus objects, it is very important to have an *ecological sample* (see p. 62) which is representative of the population of persons to whom we will generalize the results of our experiments. For example, if we had chosen highly intelligent scientists with high foreheads and thick glasses, for half our sample of stimulus objects, and idiots who had been specially selected because of their low foreheads, for the other half of our sample, how would the results of an experiment like the one in Figure 6–4A have turned out?

Social
Perception
and
Communication

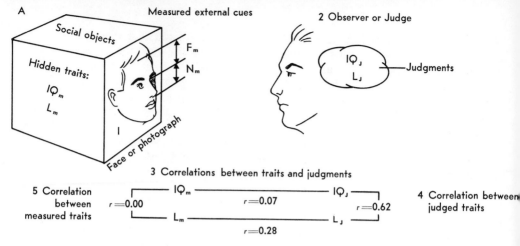

A

Social objects

Measured external cues

Hidden traits:

IQ_m

L_m

Face or photograph

2 Observer or Judge

IQ_J

L_J

Judgments

5 Correlation
between
measured traits

3 Correlations between traits and judgments

IQ_m ————————— IQ_J

$r=0.00$ $r=0.07$ $r=0.62$

L_m ————————— L_J

$r=0.28$

4 Correlation between
judged traits

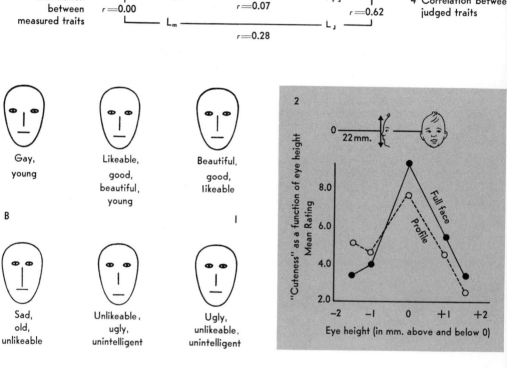

B

Gay,
young

Likeable,
good,
beautiful,
young

Beautiful,
good,
likeable

I

Sad,
old,
unlikeable

Unlikeable,
ugly,
unintelligent

Ugly,
unlikeable,
unintelligent

2

0   22mm.

"Cuteness" as a function of eye height

Mean Rating

Full face

Profile

8.0

6.0

4.0

2.0

−2   −1   0   +1   +2

Eye height (in mm. above and below 0)

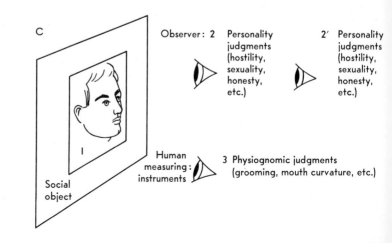

C

Social
object

I

Observer: 2 Personality
judgments
(hostility,
sexuality,
honesty,
etc.)

2′ Personality
judgments
(hostility,
sexuality,
honesty,
etc.)

Human
measuring:
instruments

3 Physiognomic judgments
(grooming, mouth curvature, etc.)

Figure 6-4. Judging intelligence and other traits from photographs. The task of judging traits from faces is similar to that of judging distance from the depth cues (p. 50). (A) Photographs of 46 soldiers (the social objects) (1) were rated by 25 judges (2) to obtain judgments of intelligence, IQ_j, likeability, L_j, and other traits (Brunswik). The actual measured IQ's of the soldiers, IQ_m, and their own judgments about each other's likeability, L_m, could then be compared with the observers' judgments of these qualities, and with measurements of each soldier's features, such as his height of forehead, F_m, or length of nose, N_m. The extent to which these measures and judgments agree with one another was measured by the correlation coefficient, r, in which a value of 1.00 means perfect agreement and 0.00 means no agreement whatsoever. At (3) we see that measured and judged IQ's did not correspond to any appreciable degree, but that we did obtain a halo effect: If observers rated a soldier as intelligent, they also tended to rate him as likeable, and vice versa, as indicated by the correlation between IQ_j and L_j at (4). This correlation is not veridical, since there is no corresponding agreement between IQ_m and L_m (5). The halo effect is a type of response bias that is particularly prevalent in social perception, and acts as a kind of prejudice that someone who is endowed with one good trait will also have other good traits—if there is no other basis for deciding about the latter.

(B) Because it is difficult to vary the features (the measured external cues, such as F_m and N_m in (A)) when using persons or their photographs as social objects, schematic drawings have been used instead to discover the contribution made by different spacing of facial features to judgments of intelligence, age, character, and so on (1) (Brunswik et al.), and the effects of varying eye-position on qualities such as cuteness (2) (Brooks et al.). This solution is limited, however, to those facial cues that can be readily manipulated and measured. A less restrictive procedure is illustrated at (C).

(C) Faces differ from one another in ways that are difficult or impossible to measure in inches or millimeters, but we can still try to discover the specific stimulus features that are responsible for different perceptions of personality. Suppose that two different samples of observers, (2) and (2'), show close agreement in their judgments of a set of photographs (or of other social objects), (1); that is, those objects that one group considers to be high in hostility, are also judged high in hostility by the other group, and those judged to be low in honesty by one group, are also so judged by the other (in fact, correlation coefficients do range between 0.36 to 0.98 for a number of judged personality traits). This implies that there are features of the objects to which both groups of judges are responding in the same way, and it is then our task to discover what those features are. (Note how similar this problem is to the search for the effective stimuli in form perception, p. 89; it is a procedure that arises whenever we start with a reliable set of perceptual responses first, and then wish to discover the particular stimuli producing them.) To discover the features that are responsible for the perceived traits, still another group of observers (3) may be employed; this time, however, they serve as human measuring instruments, since all we want from them is their judgment of such features as the relative grooming, mouth curvature, complexion, and so forth, for each social object—measures which would be extremely difficult if not impossible to obtain with purely physical instruments. By such procedures, we find that wearing glasses imparts intelligence, dependability, and industriousness; lips that are relaxed, of more than average thickness, or heavily lipsticked, cause a woman to seem highly sexual; and so forth (Secord et al.).

expressions of emotional states (Fig. 6-5A). The milder forms of facial communication have scarcely been explored, but it seems that there are in fact unitary segments of expression that can be combined into longer sequences in different ways (Figure 6-5B).

Let us now return to the question of how we judge character traits from

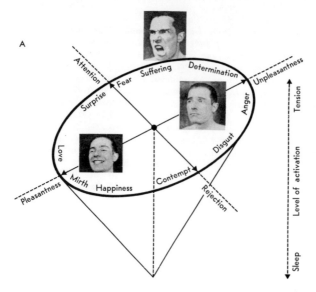

Figure 6-5. *Facial expressions of feelings and intentions. Since Leonardo da Vinci, various rules for conveying emotions by different facial contortions have been proposed (in unpleasant moods, the mouth turns downward, while in pleasant ones, it turns upward, and so forth). Although judges may not agree on the precise name to be given to any posed or unposed photograph of an emotional expression, they can place such photographs with considerable reliability on a three-dimensional scale (A), which runs from attention to rejection, pleasantness to unpleasantness, and sleep to tension (Schlosberg). It appears, therefore, that any static emotional expression may be described completely in terms of its share of each of these three qualities, much as any patch of color can be described in terms of its hue, saturation, and brightness (p. 20).*

(B) In the social intercourse of real life, in the social communication of the stage and screen, and in the animated cartoon that cuts across all cultures to capture the interest of sophisticate and savage alike, we are confronted by continually changing expressions, not by static photographs. In order to analyze this flow of social communication, we shall need some appropriate unit of analysis. A bare start in this direction has been made by showing judges motion pictures of

faces and their pictures. Since the natural or habitual arrangement of any person's features is likely to be closer to the contortions produced by some expressions than to others, it is to this that we may be responding when we perceive character traits—to the incipient emotion, desire, or intention each face seems about to express, however faintly.*

These are relatively pale social qualities, however. People are also looked at for their own sakes, not only to learn whether they are honest, how intelligent they are, or whether they are about to disagree with what we are saying. Attractiveness and repulsiveness, and other powerful physiognomic qualities, are immediately experienced properties, not judgments about character traits in any simple sense.

Esthetic Qualities and the Attractiveness of Social Objects and Events.　　Works of art are contemplated for their esthetic qualities, of course, but both people and commercial products may also have esthetic value as their single most

---

*We may well learn about facial expressions as early as we learn to perceive spatial form, so that any curve or line would be expected to have some social meaning by virtue of its relationship to some class of expressions. A number of experiments have demonstrated that meaningless curves and jagged lines do in fact communicate "physiognomic" properties (for instance, warm, happy, friendly vs. cold, sad, unfriendly), but we do not as yet know whether they do so in ways which would fit this hypothesis.

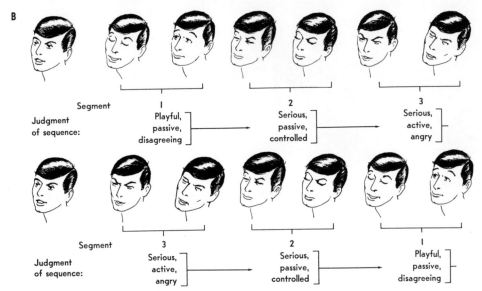

B

Segment	1	2	3
Judgment of sequence:	Playful, passive, disagreeing	Serious, passive, controlled	Serious, active, angry

Segment	3	2	1
Judgment of sequence:	Serious, active, angry	Serious, passive, controlled	Playful, passive, disagreeing

conversations, and allowing them to stop the action each time the actor's face changes from expressing one intention or feeling to another. That judges showed a very great deal of agreement at this task is promising with respect to the existence of such units. When drawings of the middle and end frames of each of these expressive segments were extracted from the movie (such as 1, 2, and 3, above) and combined into sequences in different orders, the social qualities of each segment remained the same regardless of the sequence in which it was embedded, which is promising with respect to the stability of these units. It still remains to be determined whether the three dimensions shown in (A) are as sufficient to describe the flow of expression as they are for static photographs.

important characteristic. Beauty and ugliness may be only skin-deep, but they affect our lives in untold ways. Marriage and careers depend heavily on facial beauty or attractiveness. Multibillion-dollar cosmetic and fashion industries exist to achieve it, and equally mammoth advertising and TV industries are designed to display these and other packaging skills. The automotive industry sells visual attractiveness as much as it sells horsepower. Children work hard to get comic books, admissions run high in the more genteel forms of burlesque, and even fish will do work for the reward of seeing other fish (Figure 6-6A). We know very little about these properties as yet.

Observers usually agree quite well about what is attractive or unattractive, so that it is reasonable to hope that we can discover the stimulus bases for these immensely important qualities (Figure 6-4B, C). To what uses would we put such information? Sheer measurement of the pleasingness of one person or object as compared to another has, of course, almost immediate commercial application in the "packaging and marketing" of people (in entertainment or in politics) and of commodities. These enterprises are run today by intuition alone, but, to the extent that imagination or art can in fact produce consistent results, we may hope for equal success by scientific analysis and, perhaps, for eventual understanding of the underlying psychological laws involved. We have touched upon one possible contributory factor above, in terms of the emotions any expression may suggest. An example of a law

Social
Perception
and
Communication

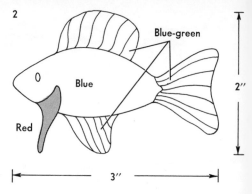

A1

Figure 6-6. **Esthetic qualities and the attractiveness of social stimuli.** *(A) We know that man, as well as the lower animals, will do work to gain rewards of food and drink—to gain the necessities of life. Both beast and man will also do work simply to gain the reward of seeing (or hearing, or touching) certain stimuli. The male Siamese fighting fish (1), which will fight any male intruding on its territory, can be conditioned to perform some task, such as swimming through a ring, to obtain the reward of seeing the model (2) of another male (Thompson). (B) With human beings, the list of stimuli that are rewarding to perceive runs from Mozart symphonies to Miss America, from Picasso paintings to popular tunes. Except for some arbitrary beauty-contest conventions about "ideal" female dimensions, however, we know less about attractive stimuli for man that we do about those for fish.*

(C) There have been many attempts to discover the formulas for esthetic value, to find the laws that will tell us what stimulus pattern will be pleasing or attractive. A very interesting one of recent vintage is the "butterfly curve" shown here, which is intended to apply to various stimuli (McClelland et al.). The vertical line (1) is the adaptation level, *or the stimulation we are habituated to (Helson). According to this curve, a stimulus at adaptation level—say, bath water at body temperature—will be neither pleasing nor unpleasing: It will be neutral (2). As the stimulus departs from the adaptation level slightly—say, by becoming slightly warmer or cooler than 98.6°—it will become pleasant to experience (3, 3') (Haber). As the stimulus becomes still more different from the adaptation level, it will become unpleasant and noxious (4, 4'). Although evidence is insufficient to evaluate this theory as yet, think about the cycle of unpopularity, popularity, and neutrality through which popular songs (and other fashion cycles) swing.*

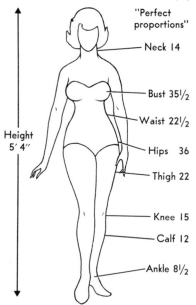

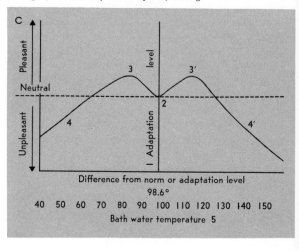

B

that attempts to predict esthetic quality or pleasantness-unpleasantness is shown in Figure 6-6C. There are many theories of esthetics; whether any is valid, however, can only be answered after far more research than has yet been undertaken.

Perception and Action

The aspects of the per-
ceived world with which we dealt in the first five chapters were, in general, conditions for behavior in this sense: If you want to get from *here* to *there*, your perception of the intervening space will help decide what path you take. Occasionally, a much stronger incentive to action is involved, as when imminent collision (p. 95) elicits an involuntary wince. In general, however, the qualities of the physical world do not themselves compel us to act in one way or another. The qualities of social perception, on the other hand, have much more of a *demand character*, meaning that they themselves are frequently goals or goads to action. As we see, so we do—this connection between perception and behavior is much closer, when it is social qualities we are studying.

What these scattered patches of research and hypotheses mark out, then, is a junction point, at which the study of perception, long concerned only with explaining our experiences, rejoins the mainstream of psychology proper and promises to become an important tool in the prediction and control of behavior.

Selected Readings

Two recently published textbooks on perception are particularly relevant for Chapters 1–4: S. H. Bartley, *Principles of perception* (New York: Harper & Row, 1958), and W. N. Dember, *Psychology of perception* (New York: Holt, Rinehart, and Winston, 1960). A set of journal reprints, recommended for supplementing Chapters 4 and 5, appears in *Readings in perception,* edited by D. C. Beardslee and M. Wertheimer (Princeton: Van Nostrand, 1958); many of the papers listed under *Illustration Credits and References* (p. 115) are contained in this collection. More detailed discussion of topics covered in each chapter can be found in the following sources:

Chapters 1–3

Osgood, C. E. *Method and theory in experimental psychology.* New York: Oxford University Press, 1953, chapters 1–4.

Woodworth, R. S., and H. Schlosberg. *Experimental psychology.* New York: Holt, Rinehart, and Winston, 1954, chapters 8–13.

Chapter 4

Hebb, D. O. *The organization of behavior.* New York: Wiley, 1949, chapters 1–5.

Postman, L. (ed.). *Psychology in the making.* New York: Knopf, 1962, chapter 5.

Osgood, C. E. *Method and theory in experimental psychology,* chapters 5–7.

Woodworth, R. S., and H. Schlosberg. *Experimental psychology,* chapters 14–16.

Chapter 5

Attneave, F. *Applications of information theory to psychology.* New York: Holt, Rinehart, and Winston, 1959, chapter 4.

Gibson, J. J. *The perception of the visual world.* Boston: Houghton Mifflin, 1950.

Koffka, K. *Principles of Gestalt psychology.* New York: Harcourt, Brace, 1935, chapters 3–6.

Chapter 6

Heider, F. *The psychology of interpersonal relations.* New York: Wiley, 1958, chapters 1–3.

Lambert, W. W., and W. E. Lambert. *Social psychology.* Englewood Cliffs, N. J.: Prentice-Hall, 1964, chapter 3.

Tagiuri, R., and L. Petrullo (eds.). *Person perception and interpersonal behavior.* Stanford: Stanford University Press, 1958.

Woodworth, R. S., and H. Schlosberg. *Experimental psychology,* chapter 5.

Illustration Credits
and References

Chapter 1. *1–2A:* After E. Boring. A new ambiguous figure. *Amer. J. Psychol.*, 1930, 42, 444. *1–2C:* Photo by H. H. Pittman from National Audubon Society. *1–2D:* Photo from Wide World Photos.

Chapter 3. *3–7:* Courtesy Eastman Kodak Company. *3–9A:* Courtesy Eastman Kodak Company. *3–10:* L. Hurvich and D. Jameson. An opponent-process theory of color vision. *Psychol. Rev.*, 1957, 64, 384–404. *3–11:* After H. Asher. *The seeing eye.* London: Duckworth, 1961.

Chapter 4. *4–2:* C. Perky. *Amer. J. Psychol.*, 1910, 23, 422–452. *4–6:* B. Julesz. Binocular depth perception of computer-generated patterns. *The Bell System Tech. J.*, 1960, 39, 1125–1162. Thanks are due to Dr. Benjamin White of M.I.T. for furnishing the random dot matrix used as the starting point to produce 4–6B1. *4–10B:* H. Witkin, H. Lewis, M. Hertzman, K. Machover, P. Meissner, and S. Wapner. *Personality through perception.* New York: Harper, 1954. *4–12A:* E. Thorndike. The instinctive reactions of young chicks. *Psychol. Rev.*, 1899, 6, 282–291. *4–12B:* E. Gibson and R. Walk. The "visual cliff." *Sci. Amer.*, 1960, 202, 64–71. Photo by William Vandivert. R. Walk and S. Dodge. Visual depth perception of a 10-month-old monocular human infant. *Sci.*, 1962, 134, 1692. *4–13:* R. Held and A Hein. Movement produced stimulation in the development of visually guided behavior. *J. comp. Psychol.*, 1963, 56, 872–876. *4–17:* W. Ittelson and F. Kilpatrick. Experiments in perception. *Sci. Amer.*, 1952, 185, 50–55. *4–17C:* Photo from The Institute for International Social Research, Princeton, N. J. *4–21A:* A. Holway and E. Boring. The moon illusion and the angle of regard. *Amer. J. Psychol.*, 1940, 53, 109–116. *4–21B:* L. Kaufman and I. Rock. The moon illusion. *Sci. Amer.*, 1962, 207, 120–130. *4–21C:* W. King and H. Gruber. Moon illusion and Emmert's law. *Sci.*, 1962, 135, 1125–1126. *4–22A:* After W. Köhler. *Gestalt psychology.* New York: Liveright, 1929. *4–22B:* After W. Metzger. *Gesetze des Sehens.* Frankfurt: Kramer, 1953.

4–22C: E. Brunswik. *Perception and the representative design of psychological experiments.* Berkeley: University of California Press, 1956. *4–22D:* Photo courtesy of the American Museum of Natural History. *4–26:* D. Hebb. *Organization of behavior.* New York: Wiley, 1949. D. Hubel and T. Wiesel. Receptive fields, binocular interaction and functional architecture in the cat's visual cortex. *J. Physiol.*, 1962, 160, 106–154. *4–27:* Adapted from D. Hebb. *A textbook of psychology.* Philadelphia: Saunders, 1958, 102, 104. *4–28A1:* W. Köhler and H. Wallach. Figural after-effects, an investigation of visual process. *Proc. Amer. Philos. Soc.*, 1944, 88, 269–357. *4–28A2:* J. Gibson. Adaptation, after-effect and contrast in the perception of curved lines. *J. exp. Psychol.*, 1933, 16, 1–31. J. Krauskopf. Figural after-effects with a stabilized retinal image. *Amer J. Psychol.*, 1960, 73, 294–297. *4–28A3:* J. Gibson and F. Backlund. An after-effect in haptic space perception. *Quart. J. exp. Psychol.*, 1963, 15, 145–153. *4–28B:* I. Kohler. Experiments with goggles. *Sci Amer.*, 1962, 206, 62–72. H. Mikaelian and R. Held. Two types of adaptation to an optically rotated visual field. *Amer. J. Psychol.*, in press. *4–28C:* After R. Leeper. A study of a neglected portion of the field of learning: the development of sensory organization. *J. genet. Psychol.*, 1935, 46, 41–75. *4–28D:* M. Henle. An experimental investigation of past experiences as a determinant of visual form perception. *J. exp. Psychol.*, 1942, 30, 1–22. W. Hayes. J. Robinson, and L. Brown. An effect of past experience on perception: an artifact. *Amer. Psychol.*, 1961, 16, 420 (abstr.). *4–28E:* This informal experiment is based on unpublished research conducted with similar stimuli by Professors J. J. Gibson and E. J. Gibson.

Chapter 5. *5–1A:* H. Wallach. Brightness constancy and the nature of achromatic colors. *J. exp Psychol.*, 1948, 38, 310–324. *5–1B:* C. Hess and H. Pretori. Messende Versuche über die Gesetzmässigkeit des simultanen Helligkeitskontrastes. *Arch. Augenheil.*, 1894, 40, 14. D. Jameson and L. Hurvich. Theory of brightness and color contrast in human vision.

Vis. Res., in press. *5–1C:* J. Hochberg and J. Beck. Apparent spatial arrangement and perceived brightness. *J. exp. Psychol.*, 1954, 47, 263–266. *5–2B:* E. Land. Color vision and the natural image. *Proc. Natl. Acad. Sci.*, 1959, 45, 115–129. *5–3A:* W. Ittelson and F. Kilpatrick. Experiments in perception. *Sci Amer.*, 1952, 185, 50–55. *5–3B:* W. Gogel, B. Hartman, and G. Harker. The retinal size of a familiar object as a determiner of apparent distance. *Psychol. Monogr.*, 1957, 71 (#442), 1–16. W. Epstein. The known-size apparent-distance hypothesis. *Amer. J. Psychol.*, 1961, 74, 333–346. *5–4B:* I. Rock and S. Ebenholtz. The relational determination of perceived size. *Psychol. Rev.*, 1959, 66, 387. *5–5:* H. Wallach and V. McKenna. On size-perception in the absence of cues for distance. *Amer. J. Psychol.*, 1960, 73, 458–460. *5–6:* Based on J. Gibson. *The perception of the visual world.* Boston: Houghton Mifflin, 1950. *5–7A through I:* Based on J. Gibson. *Ibid.*, 88–94. *5–7J:* O. Smith and P. Smith. An illusion of parallelism. *Perc. mot. Skills*, 1962, 15, 455–461. *5–8D:* L. Penrose and R. Penrose. Impossible objects: a special type of visual illusion. *Brit. J. Psychol.*, 1958, 49, 31–33. The particular picture shown here is from J. Hochberg. The psychophysics of pictorial perception. *Audio-Vis. Comm. Rev.*, 1962, 10, 22–54. *5–8E:* Patterned after several designs by M. C. Escher. *The graphic work of M. C. Escher.* New York, Duell, Sloan and Pearce, 1960. *5–8F:* J. Hochberg and V. Brooks. Pictorial recognition as an unlearned ability: a study of one child's performance. *Amer. J. Psychol.*, 1962, 75, 624–628. *5–8G:* R. Zimmermann and J. Hochberg. Pictorial recognition in the infant monkey. *Proc. Psychonomics Soc.*, 1963, 46 (abstr.). *5–9:* Max Wertheimer. Principles of perceptual organization (tr. by Michael Wertheimer). In D. Beardslee and M. Wertheimer. *Readings in perception.* Princeton: Van Nostrand, 1958, 115–135. K. Koffka. *Principles of Gestalt psychology.* New York: Harcourt, Brace, 1935. W. Köhler. *Gestalt psychology.* New York: Liveright, 1929. *5–10:* H. Kopfermann. Psychologische Untersuchungen über die Wirkung zweidimensionaler Darstellungen körperlicher Gebilde. *Psychol. Forsch.*, 1930, 13, 293–364. *5–12B:* J. Hochberg and V. Brooks. The psychophysics of form: reversible-perspective drawings of spatial objects. *Amer. J. Psychol.*, 1960, 73, 337–354. *5–12C:* F. Attneave. Some informational aspects of visual perception. *Psychol. Rev.*, 1954, 61, 183–193. *5–14:* G. Johansson. *Configurations in event perception.* Uppsala: Almquist and Wiksell, 1950. *5–15A:* H. Wallach and D. O'Connell. The kinetic depth effect. *J. exp. Psychol.*, 1948, 38, 310–324. *5–15B:* Adapted from J. Gibson. *The perception of the visual world.* Boston: Houghton Mifflin, 1950. *5–16:* After J. Gibson, P. Olum, and F. Rosenblatt. Parallax and perspective during aircraft landings. *Amer. J. Psychol.*, 1955, 68, 372–385. *5–17:* After J. Gibson. *Ibid.* (5–15B). *5–18:*

K. Smith and W. Smith. *Perception and motion.* Philadelphia: Saunders, 1962.

Chapter 6. *6–1A:* J. Bruner and C. Goodman. Value and need as organizing factors in perception. *J. abn. soc. Psychol.*, 1947, 42, 33–44. W. Lambert, R. Solomon, and P. Watson. Reinforcement and extinction as factors in size estimation. *J. exp. Psychol.*, 1949, 39, 637–641. L. Carter and K. Schooler. Value, need, and other factors in perception. *Psychol. Rev.*, 1949, 56, 200–207. *6–1B1, 2:* R. Levine, I. Chein, and G. Murphy. The relation of the intensity of a need to the amount of perceptual distortion: a preliminary report. *J. Psychol.*, 1942, 13, 283–293. R. Schafer and G. Murphy. The role of autism in a visual figure-ground relationship. *J. exp. Psychol.*, 1943, 32, 335–343. D. McClelland and J. Atkinson. The projective expression of needs. I. The effect of different intensities of the hunger drive on perception. *J. Psychol.*, 1948, 25, 205–222. *6–1B3:* E. McGinnies. Emotionality and perceptual defense. *Psychol. Rev.*, 1949, 16, 244–251. R. Lazarus and R. McCleary. Autonomic discrimination without awareness: an experiment on subception. *Psychol. Rev.*, 1951, 58, 113–122. *6–2A:* J. Gibson and A. Pick. Perception of another person's looking behavior. *Amer. J. Psychol.*, 1963, 76, 386–394. *6–2B:* After F. Heider and M. Simmel. An experimental study of apparent behavior. *Amer. J. Psychol.*, 1944, 57, 243–259. *6–3A:* C. Lombroso and G. Ferrero. *La femme criminelle et la prostituée.* Paris: Germer Baillière, 1896. *6–3B:* After W. H. Sheldon and W. B. Tucker. *The varieties of human physique.* New York: Harper, 1940. *6–4A:* E. Brunswik. *Ibid.* (4–22C). *6–4B:* E. Brunswik and L. Reiter. Eindrucks-Charactere schematisierter Gesichter. *Zeitschr. f. Psychol.*, 1937, 142, 67–134. V. Brooks and J. Hochberg. A psychophysical study of "cuteness." *Perc. mot. Skills*, 1960, 11, 205. *6–4C:* P. Secord. Facial features and inference processes in interpersonal perception. In R. Tagiuri and L. Petrullo (eds.). *Person perception and interpersonal behavior.* Stanford: Stanford University Press, 1958, 310–315. P. Secord and J. Muthard. Personalities in faces: IV. A descriptive analysis of the perception of women's faces and the identification of some physiognomic determinants. *J. Psychol.*, 1955, 39, 269–278. *6–5:* H. Schlosberg. The description of facial expressions in terms of two dimensions. *J. exp. Psychol.*, 1952, 44, 235. *6–6A1:* New York Zoological Society Photo. *6–6A2:* T. Thompson. Visual reinforcement in Siamese Fighting Fish. *Sci.*, 1963, 141, 55–57. Copyright 1963 by the American Association for the Advancement of Science. *6–6B:* D. McClelland, J. Atkinson, R. Clark, and E. Lowell. *The achievement motive.* New York: Appleton-Century-Crofts, 1953. H. Helson. *Adaptation level theory.* New York: Harper & Row, 1964. R. Haber. Discrepancy from adaptation level as a source of affect. *J. exp. Psychol.*, 1958, 56, 370–384.

Index